Visas for Life

P. Sugihara

杉原弘樹

1995. 12. 15.

Visas for Life
by Yukiko Sugihara

Translated by Hiroki Sugihara
with Anne Hoshiko Akabori

Introduction by
Sir Edmund L. de Rothschild

Edited by Lani Silver and Eric Saul
Holocaust Oral History Project

PRE-PUBLICATION COPY
55th Anniversary Commemorative Edition

*This book is dedicated to
my beloved husband, Chiune,
my dear sister Setsuko, and
my third son Haruki,
whom I think of every day.*

Photographs courtesy of the Sugihara Family;
Setsuko Kikuchi; Yad Vashem, Jerusalem, Israel;
the Holocaust Oral History Project, San Francisco; Eric Saul;
the United States Holocaust Memorial Museum, Washington,
DC; Taisho Publishing Company, Tokyo; Ron Greene;
David Granat; Art Waldinger/Simon Wiesenthal Center;
Michael Loeb.

Book design by Nigel French, Small World Productions.
Printing by Edwards Brothers, Inc.
Copyright © 1993 Yukiko Sugihara
English Translation Copyright © 1995 Edu-Comm. Plus
236 West Portal #249
San Francisco, CA 94127
ISBN 0-9649674-0-5

*"If you save the life of one person,
it is as if you saved the world entire."*
— *Jewish Proverb*

*"Even a hunter cannot kill a bird
that comes to him for refuge."*
— *Japanese Proverb*

Table of Contents

Foreward 8
Preface 9
Prologue 10

The People Who Escaped 1
The Chilly Summer 1
Issuing the Visas 20

Life in Europe 31
Our First Meeting 31
The Departure 42
The Country of the Midnight Sun 46

The Dark Cloud 53
Berlin 53
The Stream of Moldau 56
The Small Island That Surprised Europe 61
The Destruction of Berlin 66

A Foreboding of Defeat 71
The King Who Had Forgotten How to Laugh 71
Escape Through a Smoke Screen 79
In the Bombardment 86
Diplomats of a Defeated Country 92

The Internment 97
Days of Anxiety 97
The Endless Journey 100
Hope 103

Bitter Suffering in Our Homeland 107
Advised to Resign 107
A Second Life 112
In a Faraway Country 117

Reunion 123
A Sudden Telephone Call 123
The Golden Hill 128
Friends All Over the World 135
Worn-Out Visas 137

Appendix, November 1995 144
Chiune Sugihara Chronology 146
List of Sugihara Awards 149
Acknowledgements 151

Foreward

I AM INDEED honored to have been asked to write a foreword to Mrs. Yukiko Sugihara's book. She was the wife of the renowned Consul Chiune Sugihara, the Japanese diplomat to Lithuania who, in August 1940, was instrumental in saving the lives of approximately 6,000 Jewish people. Had he not issued the visas and documents, these people would have perished. Mrs. Sugihara has faithfully described the extremes of life under the regimes of Finland, Lithuania, Germany, Czechoslovakia and Romania. She has portrayed her faith in her husband's superb efforts; she describes her trials and tribulations which they endured, some anxious, some happy.

It was in Romania that the Sugiharas found themselves at the end of the war when Japan had been defeated and lay in ruins. The Sugihara family's extraordinary journey back to Japan and his subsequent abrupt dismissal from the Japanese Foreign Office is vividly recounted. Mrs. Yukiko Sugihara's strength of character shines. We learn of the subsequent gratitude shown to her and her husband by those people they had saved. Many people who received visas were never able to adequately express their gratitude to Mr. Sugihara.

Officially no permission was given to Chiune Sugihara to issue the visas to freedom and safety. It is ironic that it was later discovered that the Japanese Foreign Office had in its files a study of the Jewish people and their culture which gave a favorable report. Perhaps as a result of this report, the Jewish refugees who were in Shanghai and elsewhere in the Far East were never handed back to the Nazis, despite repeated requests by the Germans.

This book is a historical record of Consul Sempo Sugihara's epic humanitarianism, which has had the recognition of the Jewish community worldwide.

Sir Edmund L. de Rothschild
August 1993

Preface

IN THE SPRING of 1991 I had a very serious illness. I was so sick that I feared I would not live. As I reviewed my life, I reminisced about my childhood. Suddenly I was in my father's consulate office in Lithuania looking down at the crowd. I remembered the sad eyes of the Jewish refugees and I felt very sad. As I lay in my hospital bed, I felt that if I were to recover, I would tell my father's story to the world.

At that time, in the spring of 1991, hardly anyone knew about the actions of my father in Lithuania during the war. My mother had just turned 77 years old. Because she had always been a writer and a poet, she had kept notes about her life in Europe. I felt that we needed to encourage her to write down her memories, especially about her days in Kaunas with my father. So with encouragement from her family and friends, she decided to write this book. She was also encouraged by the public's interest in this story.

This book was difficult for my mother to write. My mother was raised in an era when people did not talk about their accomplishments. In my mother's time, people were also taught to keep their feelings to themselves. So my mother tells her story here a bit reluctantly and humbly. Therefore, this account is an expression of her willingness to share her experiences and feelings, so that the world does not repeat its mistakes. This is the viewpoint of a woman who grew up in a different time. She is a product of that time. These memories are her gift to the world. They are presented as honestly and forthrightly as she was able to do.

I have attempted to translate my mother's experiences as written in her Japanese version and as she conveyed them to me. Although I attended City College in Sacramento as a young man, my English may not be as flawless as I would like it to be. I apologize for any shortcomings that may appear in this book.

Hiroki Sugihara, November 1995

Prologue

"WE WOULD LIKE to make a movie about Mr. Sugihara. Do you think you will have a chance to visit the U.S.?" a film company executive in Hollywood inquired in 1990. They asked for details about the life of my husband, Chiune Sugihara.

In the years since my husband had passed away, I began compiling his notes and memoirs, adding my own recollections about our family experiences during World War II and its aftermath. To ensure that these events would be preserved and remembered, I realized I should act quickly. I was the only person in a position to remember our important story.

As I looked through Chiune's notes, his memoirs reawakened my own memories of the events which occurred in Kaunas in 1940. I realized I should act quickly while I was still able to undertake this task. Receiving this letter from the movie producer encouraged me to continue to pursue my goal to retell our story with renewed vigor.

Chiune tells part of our story in his notebooks. The story began to unfold on a gloomy morning in late July 1940. The drastic change in season was already evident, as is typical of northern European countries. At 6:00 a.m., my attention was directed to the sound of excited voices. As the clamor outside grew, I realized the disturbance originated at the front gate of our consulate, which faced the street. We lived in Kaunas, Lithuania, where my husband had been recently assigned the position of Deputy Consul General. My three sons, my sister, Chiune, and I had been there for nine months.

Upon Chiune's unexpected and sudden reassignment to this new post in Lithuania, instead of his original appointment in Turkey, we arrived in Kaunas in November 1939. This change in post, this twist of fate, we later realized, affected the lives of thousands of Jews.

As Chiune and I looked through the curtains, we saw a large crowd of people There were approximately 100 or more young and old men and women as well as children, looking frightened, disheveled, and very agitated. In his recollections, Chiune described the expression on those faces as one of desperation. I, too, vividly remember this. I shall never forget the sight of the frightened children clinging to their mothers. We soon discovered that the people standing at the gate were Jewish refugees who had just escaped from Poland to Lithuania. Looking at Chiune, I understood that my husband quickly grasped the impact of the situation, and realized the seriousness of their plight and the conditions causing these frantic attempts to see him. The refugees wanted transit visas that would allow them to leave Europe through Russia and Japan.

The unstable political climate of these very uncertain times in Europe, as in most parts of the world, brought daily changes. Adolf Hitler had just concluded a Nonaggression Pact with the Soviet Union. This pact stipulated that Germany would divide Poland with the Soviet Union. This also resulted in the Soviet annexation of Lithuania, Estonia, and Latvia. Ten days later, on September 1, 1939, the Nazis invaded Poland. I learned that my family's new life in Kaunas coincided with the onset of World War II. By the following spring, Lithuania was overrun by Soviet troops.

We witnessed a growing presence of Soviet soldiers in Kaunas; an eerie atmosphere of uneasy quiet pervaded our new city. A sense of foreboding and apprehension had settled over Kaunas, as it had in Europe. Each morning when I woke up, I hoped nothing bad would happen to us.

In his notes, Chiune indicated that he worried about the brutality of the Nazis in their occupation of Western Poland. He documented the daily worsening of the situation and his belief that the Jews were suffering cruelly at the hands of the Nazis. As the situation became even more desperate, some Jews banded together and migrated northward, fleeing for their lives. They overcame indescribable suffering and hardships on their way to Kaunas before arriving outside the gate of our consulate.

The actions my husband took over the following months were later referred to as "The Incident in Lithuania" by the inner circle of people connected with the Japanese Foreign Ministry. We decided, against the instructions of Japan, to issue thousands of transit visas to the Jews who were fleeing Poland. In the years that followed, Chiune, the children, and I did not discuss what we had done in Kaunas. In our hearts we believed we had made the correct and only possible choice at that time. When we returned home after the war, Chiune was dismissed from the diplomatic service. He told that it was because of the "Incident in Lithuania."

In April 1989, I received an invitation from a Jewish organization in New York to visit the United States with my eldest son, Hiroki. During our stay in New York, I wanted to travel to Chicago to see Mrs. Rochelle Zell. Mrs. Zell, her husband Bernard, and their three-year-old daughter Julie, had stood in front of the consulate that fateful morning in July 1940. Her family had escaped to America via Japan because of the visa they received from Chiune. Later, Mrs. Zell and I began writing one another. While we had exchanged letters for some time, this was the first time I would meet her personally. When I called her, her happy voice responded, "by all means, please visit." Hiroki went to visit his friends in other parts of the United States, while I went to Chicago to visit Mrs. Zell.

Upon arrival in Chicago, I was greeted by Mrs. Zell, her daughter, and her son-in-law. Because of her ill health, I was surprised to see her at the gate of the airport. As she greeted me, she took my hands and held them tightly. She continued to do so in the car and even as we entered her beautiful home on Lake Michigan.

Mrs. Zell had gone to great lengths preparing many kinds of dishes. She cooked each dish by herself. In the glow of the setting sun on Lake Michigan, we enjoyed the food and reminisced about the past, the memories, and the passings of our husbands. We talked about the hardships both our families had endured. Chiune and Mr. Zell had died about the same time. Mrs. Zell remarked that her husband often talked about what had happened in Lithuania and his great desire to visit Chiune in Japan. We felt very comfortable speaking together in German. This intimate conversation, in a language of our past, brought us closer. I felt very happy to have met a truly special friend.

"The Incident," which is remembered not only by the Zells, but by the survivors who were in Kaunas at that time, still provides me with much mail. This "Incident" referred to a series of events that lasted approximately one month, and resulted in many precious friends like the Zell family.

Japanese Consulate, Kaunas 1940.

Chapter 1

The People Who Escaped

The Chilly Summer

THE EVENTS THAT UNFOLDED on the morning of July 27, 1940, are still very vivid and clearly imprinted in my mind. On that morning, my husband, Chiune Sugihara, and I had a light breakfast, and as was his custom, Chiune went downstairs to his office. Always an early riser, he began his day at dawn with a chorus of birds. That morning was a beautiful one, as fresh, gentle sunshine streamed in through the windows. Although it was summer and the sun filtered into the room through the curtains, it was very chilly. The temperature was about 59° which is not unusual in Northern European countries. Despite the early morning chill, it was comfortable in the consulate because the heater was set to go on before we awoke.

We had been living in a lovely section of Kaunas for about nine months. Kaunas was a nice quiet city, with rows of old-fashioned houses. The Japanese Consulate was halfway up a hill, giving us a complete view of the city from our garden. The consulate was surrounded by beautiful large homes and lush gardens. Our family lived on the first and second floors of the building; the half-basement served as my husband's office. A brother and sister, two Lithuanian students, lived upstairs from us on the third floor. None of the consulate employees lived in the consulate building.

My husband's usual routine was to go downstairs after breakfast and reappear at lunch. I would spend the morning reading in my room. On that morning, however, our habits and routines were to change forever.

After reading about ten lines, my husband knocked on the door and came in excitedly. He had never come up to the house during his office hours. His sudden appearance surprised me because he usually kept to his daily habits. Being a serious and disciplined person, he was faithful to routine.

"Take a look out the window, Yukiko," Chiune urged me, as he opened the curtain a little. I walked over and joined him. I could not comprehend the sight before me. The front of the consulate was surrounded by a crowd of people. There must have been 100 or 200 people in front of our house! This was indeed an extraordinary sight because our street was usually empty and always quiet. However, what I saw before me now were hundreds of people moving about, and more were coming. The sounds of the crowd grew louder and louder. People looked frightened and even desperate. They looked hungry and dirty. Some of them were climbing over the gate. It was chaotic.

The crowd was right below our window. There was a gate in front of the house. There were only a few feet between the house and the gate, so I could see everything very clearly. I could see directly into the eyes of the people waiting in front of the consulate. The images I saw that day have stayed in my mind for a lifetime. I always remember their faces and expressions. These people were terrified.

I looked at Chiune and was about to ask him what this was all about, but I stopped myself when I saw the perplexed look on his face. Chiune immediately went downstairs and soon came back with an explanation. "They're Jews; they've es-

The People Who Escaped

Jewish refugees at gate of consulate, July 1940.

caped from the Nazis. They've come from Poland and they want me to give them visas to leave the country."

Chiune considered this a serious matter, and asked one of his staff, a houseboy named Borislav, to go outside and get more information. Borislav went outside and returned. He informed us that there were more than 100 Jewish people outside and that thousands more could be expected in a few days. They were people who had fled from Poland and who had managed to escape from the Nazis. Those that escaped Nazi capture and slaughter were all heading to Kaunas, one of the only escape routes left to them. It was a migration of thousands of Jewish refugees.

Chiune described the crowd in his notebook:

"These people had walked for many days under severe conditions, dragging themselves on painful feet and enduring countless hardships. Their objective was to reach Kaunas. What they wanted was, somehow, for the Japanese Consulate to issue transit visas that would allow them to travel through the Soviet Union in order to escape the Nazis. The refugees walked regardless of the weather.

Visas for Life

Sign reads, "Jews not allowed."

> Some walked along the railroad, dragging painful feet, and some of the more fortunate rode in wagons."

According to Borislav, these people thought they could travel through the Soviet Union to the international port of Vladivostok, and then on to Japan. They had heard rumors that the Dutch and Japanese Consulates might consider issuing visas to Curacao, a Dutch colony in the Caribbean.

I remembered the sign at the entrance to the park in front of the consulate, which read in cold, authoritative German, "No Jews allowed." I knew that many Jews lived in this city and I felt repulsed seeing that anti-Semitic sign. As I remembered that sign, I felt a chill and a feeling of sadness and foreboding.

I wrote this tanka, a form of Japanese poetry, about the sign:

In harsh German
Engraved on Cold Steel
Proclaimed with an emotionless expression
Jews Forbidden

By this time, Chiune's staff had come to the consulate to confer. What I gathered from this meeting was just more uncertainty and confusion. Before I went back to my room, I reluctantly went back once again to observe the scene below.

I could see people with bloodshot eyes desperately pleading for help. I tried to stay hidden. It was apparent that they had spotted my shadow because some people began shouting and reaching out to me with their hands. Some of the men even tried to climb over the fence of the consulate, but were stopped after a brief scuffle.

I still cannot forget their eyes. They were intense and desperate. I especially remember those of the women and children. Everyone seemed very frightened. They peered into our windows, with their expressions crying out for help.

Chiune went back downstairs. I worried about my husband and strained my ears at the downstairs landing to see if I could better understand the situation.

I didn't hear my younger sister, Setsuko, come in, but suddenly she was looking over my shoulder. "I wonder what's wrong?" she said. Setsuko had come with us to Europe. She was acted as a caretaker or nanny for my children whenever we attended our many diplomatic receptions and functions.

As Setsuko observed the crowd, she began taking some pictures of the scene below. I told her, "right now, Jews in Poland, regardless of their age or sex, are rounded up, put in trucks, and taken away to ghettos or murdered." Her eyes registered shock. She said, "they are? Well, if that is the case, we must help them." She continued taking pictures.

It was an upsetting sight, and we felt badly for everyone. We saw the desperate faces of Jewish fathers and mothers holding their children in fear and anticipation. A little boy trembled. The eyes of tiny children were filled with hunger and fear. A little girl sat on the ground, worn out and frightened. I was very upset by this scene, perhaps because of my own three sons, a five-year-old, a three-year-old, and a three-month-old.

At the time, we did not have much knowledge about the European Jews. We did know, however, that they were very persecuted in Eastern Europe.

Rumors had started that in Poland people were "Jew Hunting." Attacks against Jews were occurring. This horrible expression was used to describe attacks on Jewish-owned businesses and temples, and on men, women and children. I heard that many temples were being burned. It was only after the war that I learned that Jews were taken to concentration camps like Auschwitz, where people were exterminated in unspeakable ways. At that time, it was clear that Jews who were taken by the Nazis were in grave danger.

Beginning in 1935 in Germany, the Nuremberg Laws were put into effect, and all German Jews lost their citizenship. In October 1938, tens of thousands more were forced from German borders. Because the Jews in Germany were being persecuted, they went to the foreign embassies to get visas to other countries. No one dared to help them. Their desperate situation was now explained to me by Chiune.

Chiune told me that a great wave of anti-Semitism had hit Poland when Germany invaded on September 1, 1939. This marked the beginning of World War II. The terror in Poland began then. Although anti-Semitism was by no means new to Poland, now mobile murder squads were killing Jews by the thousands. Many Jews were forced into labor gangs and were rounded up and placed in ghettos. Poland would become the home of the notorious Auschwitz concentration camp, which was built west of the city of Krakow. By the end of the war over 1.8 million people were killed there.

It was from these killings and roundups that Jews were fleeing to Lithuania for refuge. The Polish Jews who were able to escape the Nazis arrived at our doorstep in Kaunas.

Japan had signed the Japan-German Anti-Comintern Pact in November 1936. The issuance of visas to Jews might be looked upon as a hostile act against Germany. My husband and I clearly understood the severity of the situation and the danger that we would be courting if these visas were issued by him. We were aware of the possibility that we could even be executed by the Germans should Chiune issue the visas.

The People Who Escaped

The Sugihara family in Kaunas in 1939: (left to right) Setsuko Kikuchi, Chiune, Chiaki, Hiroki, and Yukiko.

As we looked at the scene below us, we contemplated our uncertain future. In my heart, I already knew what Chiune's decision would be if he had only himself to think about.

By now, Hiroki, my eldest son, who was five years old, was aware of the scene in the street below. "What do they want?" Hiroki asked me. He couldn't understand what was happening. I explained to him that all these people had come to ask for his father's help because they were in danger of being killed by some bad men. My second son, Chiaki, who had just turned three, stood next to him.

Hiroki said, "father, please help them because the poor little children need your help." I knew then that Chiune had quietly come to a decision because he understood that his family had also spoken from their hearts.

Chiaki, my second son also wanted to know if his father was going to help them. I knew then that the only right answer was, "yes, he is." Hiroki, not hearing my answer to Chiaki, pleaded to his father that he should do all he could to help the frightened children. As Hiroki and Chiaki looked on, it was obvious that, as young as my two boys were, they identified with the children below and were filled with a desire to help them.

Throughout Chiune's life, his kindness and concern for the welfare of his fellow man had been a recurrent theme. This concern was consistently the deciding factor in all of the final decisions that he made throughout his life.

For example, during his earlier career he was instrumental in acquiring the Northern Manchurian Railway System for Japan. His decision to resign his post was because of his humanitarianism. His resignation was, in reality, a protest against the ill treatment of the Chinese by the Japanese Military occupation. The Chinese later recognized his many efforts to remedy problems which they faced at this time. Later they had an opportunity to return the favor, when Chiune was negotiating the purchase of the Northern Manchurian Railroad, by providing him with some very significant information.

In July 1940, making a decision was not so simple. Making this decision was complicated by the fact that his choice would affect the whole family. It hurt me when I looked outside the window and saw a little child holding his father's hand tightly.

Because of the large crowd gathering outside, my boys could not go out to play in their favorite spot — the park across the way. So they watched the scene below from the window. It seemed to me that it wrung Hiroki's heart to see children his age facing a life-or-death situation. When Hiroki and Chiaki looked out the window, the Jews waved their hands and tried to make them laugh with funny gestures.

Men with desperate eyes continued trying to climb over fences. They overtook the maid as she tried to go out of the gate to go shopping for food. They were desperately trying to get access into the consulate to speak with Chiune. Borislav and Gudje, another officer in the consulate, had to push them away several times. This was a very disagreeable task for them.

Finally, my husband decided that the crowd could not be left standing there any longer. He asked that five Jewish representatives be chosen to speak for the crowd. Zorach Warhaftig led the five representatives. Warhaftig began to explain their situation to Chiune.

Warhaftig initiated the conversation as the four other men joined in. They all talked about how desperate they were. For the next two hours, they poured out terrible stories about the fate of Jews in Germany and Poland. They also told Chiune of their long and arduous trip from Poland to Kaunas. Chiune listened to them quietly.

Warhaftig explained how they had all narrowly escaped from Poland. They had come to Kaunas in desperation hoping to get visas at this consulate to escape from the Nazi terror. The other spokesmen emotionally described the terrible plight. Warhaftig said, "we came here because we heard that we might be able to get transit visas from the Japanese Consulate. We are asking you to issue us visas."

The crowd outside had finally settled down; with Chiune listening, there was now some hope. Even the staff in the consulate seemed to let out a sigh of relief. "Those five men told me about the horrors they would have to face if they didn't get away from the Nazis," Chiune wrote in his notebook, "and I believe them. No one would help them."

Chiune explained to them that they would have to prove that they were seeking only transit visas, not permanent visas to stay in Japan. They also had to prove their Polish citizenship. Chiune told the refugees he had recently received instructions from the Soviet government to close his office the first week of August.

The five representatives now understood that our consulate was in the process of closing. Other consulates in Lithuania had already been closed or were in the process of leaving. The representatives realized that the most crucial problem was to get valid documentation showing that they had guarantors, such as friends, relatives or acquaintances who would guarantee that they had another destination after reaching Japan. The ability to get this documentation was very important. According to Chiune's notes, their primary concern was not where they would go, but whether the Japanese Consulate would stay open long enough for them to finalize their arrangements.

The Jews asked for the Japanese transit visas because of a suggestion by a businessman, the Honorary Dutch Consul, Jan Zwartendijk, who was willing to help the Jews. Of the many consulates in Kaunas, only the Dutch Consul helped. Holland had just been occupied by Germany in May 1940, but Zwartendijk continued to issue visas to Dutch territories anyway. In reality, there was no way to go to Curacao, located in the Caribbean, except via Japan. Mr. Zwartendijk, permanently stationed in Kaunas, attended the meeting with Chiune and the five representatives. In a lighter moment during this meeting, my husband, who thought Curacao to be a somewhat obscure location, asked jokingly, "by the way, is there even a landing place in Curacao?" Mr. Zwartendijk responded quickly, "I haven't checked yet, but I'm sure that there are no customs officers there."

I have since learned that Mr. Zwartendijk took great risks to help the Jews. Furthermore, the Dutch Consul said he had received permission from his superior, Mr. L.P.J. de Decker in Riga, Latvia, to issue visas to anyone who was willing to pay a fee.

Chiune told the representatives that he could issue a few visas by his own authority, but that he could not possibly issue hundreds or even thousands of visas. He would need to get permission from the Ministry of Foreign Affairs. Since an answer could not be given, he ended the meeting for the day.

> *Chiune's Distress*
> *Being undecided*
> *About issuing the visas*
> *Tossing turning contemplating*
> *I hear his bed squeaking all night.*

That night was one of the most upsetting of Chiune's life. With the heavy burden that lay before him — should he or should he not issue the visas — it was impossible for Chiune to fall asleep. I knew that he did not sleep through the night because I heard the unceasing sound of his bed squeaking. He tossed and turned, while contemplating the situation and thinking about the decision he had to make. It was a long and sleepless night for both of us.

The next morning Chiune was distraught. "I'm going to cable the Foreign Ministry. This situation is too difficult for me to make a decision myself," he said. I sympathetically agreed with him as I replied, "please do so, because all those people out there desperately need your help." Chiune agreed.

This first cable was not sent in the usual way. It was sent as a secret document, in code, directly to the Japanese Foreign

Minister. Under normal circumstances, it would take about two weeks to send a message by ship. Sending it by cable would take only one day.

Three copies of every communiqué were required. The job of recopying Chiune's cables had become mine. I rewrote three copies of this cable by hand, careful not to make mistakes. One copy went to the Japanese Ambassador in Ger-

Visas for Life

many, another to the Japanese Ambassador in Latvia, and the third to Foreign Minister Matsuoka in Tokyo. I felt relieved when I entered the name Yosuke Matsuoka at the bottom of a page because his copy was the third and final one.

Chiune requested permission to issue the visas: "Hundreds of Jewish people have come to the consulate here in Kaunas seeking transit visas. They are suffering extremely. As a fellow human being, I cannot refuse their requests. Please permit me to issue visas to them." Formulating his request for visas as a humanitarian plea, Chiune insisted that the refugees' request for visas should not be denied.

Everyone waited impatiently for the reply, which was expected within the day. The five Jewish representatives, who had previously been selected by the crowd to represent them, anxiously came in several times to ask if any answer had been received.

The cook could not venture out to buy food because whenever the gate was opened, the crowd would try to force themselves into the consulate. I advised our cook to prepare dinner with whatever was available in the consulate.

When the reply was finally received, the answer was what Chiune had expected. His request was denied on the grounds

Yukiko and Chiaki in front of consulate.

that people without final destinations cannot be issued visas. There were events that were happening which made issuing the visas much more complicated. The Second Konoe cabinet had just been formed. The Tripartite Pact between Japan, Germany, and Italy was in the process of being completed. It was finally signed on September 27, 1940. Matsuoka, who had just replaced Hachiro Arita as Japanese Foreign Minister, was not about to permit any action which would jeopardize the formation of the Triple Alliance. Hideki Tojo had also just become Japan's Minister of War.

The cable we received read:

"CONCERNING TRANSIT VISAS REQUESTED PREVIOUSLY STOP. ADVISE ABSOLUTELY NOT TO BE ISSUED TO ANY TRAVELER NOT HOLDING FIRM END VISA WITH GUARANTEED DEPARTURE EX JAPAN STOP. NO EXCEPTIONS STOP. NO FURTHER INQUIRIES EXPECTED STOP. K TANAKA FOREIGN MINISTRY TOKYO."

The answer was 'No.' The Foreign Office clearly instructed Chiune not to issue visas to people who did not have a guaranteed destination.

For two days Chiune thought about what to do. Hundreds more Jews lined up outside the consulate. He talked about a proverb that had influenced him greatly. "Even the hunter cannot kill a bird that comes to him for refuge."

In order to better understand the situation as it was at that time, it is necessary to explain and clarify some important factors that were in effect before going further into the events that were to follow.

Originally, a Japanese Consulate in Kaunas did not exist. This post was created so that Chiune could be there to gather sensitive and crucial information for Japan about the military movements of the Soviets and the Germans. Japan felt it prudent and necessary to gather this information in order to facilitate Japan's position in the formation of the Triple Alliance with Germany and Italy.

We later found out that Chiune was not 'accidentally' sent to Lithuania. He was chosen because he was one of the only people capable of gathering the necessary information. His innate talent for languages enabled him to understand and speak fluently in both German and Russian. What better person could fulfill all the tasks necessary to reach their objectives. Actually, Chiune was originally assigned to go to Turkey, but was later reassigned to Kaunas.

Chiune was also assigned as Vice Consul rather than as Consul, in order to avoid the formalities that were associated with the post of Consul General In reality, his superior officer was Shojiro Otaka, an Ambassador Extraordinary and Plenipotentiary in Latvia. Ordinarily, protocol would dictate that he report to Otaka. Because of the unique circumstances of this situation, Chiune was told to report directly to the Foreign Office in Japan.

During the nine months we spent in Kaunas, many events occurred bringing about many changes. On August 23, 1939, the German-Soviet Nonaggression Pact was concluded. In September, Germany and the Soviet Union divided Poland between them. On October 10, the Soviet Union applied pressure on Estonia, Lithuania, and Latvia, forcing them to into a mutual assistance pact. On January 15, 1940, the Soviet Union stationed troops in Lithuania, and set up a puppet government. In May 1940, the Soviet Union revoked the pact. The Soviets then established a pro-Soviet administration, and increased their troops. In June, Lithuania was sealed off from the world and had to accept the Soviet Union conquest.

It was said that the government's leaders, including Lithuanian President Antanas Smetona, escaped to Königsberg and were interned there. The pro-Soviet administrations in the three Baltic countries decided to unite with the Soviet Union on July 21. On August 3, the unification would be approved by the Soviet Supreme Council, and Lithuania, Estonia, and Latvia would formally become part of the Soviet Union.

It was common knowledge at this time that the consulates were replete with many informants who, in reality, were spies. Many people visited our consulate, but I never could distinguish regular visitors from informants. I remember one frequent visitor that Chiune referred to as "The Crow," because he had a very dark complexion. I believed that he was a spy.

Our long family drives were also part of Chiune's job. We would go driving often. Chiune took great pleasure in driving our new and popular black Buick. After reaching our destina-

The People Who Escaped

Family outing and picnic, 1940.

tion, Chiune would drop off the children and me, and drive away by himself. He would scrupulously record everything he saw. If the population of young farmers in the area had recently decreased, it could mean they had been drafted. If the road showed deep ruts, it could indicate the movement of military equipment. Chiune also monitored ships on the river. Even a small change or an ordinary scene was telling. To avoid involving his family in a potentially dangerous situation, Chiune always kept the details to himself.

To this day, Hiroki remembers his rides with Chiune. "My father used to take us on picnics all the time. We would go to out-of-the-way places, following the tracks of tanks or trucks. My father was always looking around and taking pictures. I didn't realize this at the time, but he was gathering information on Russian and German activities."

After his request to issue visas was denied, Chiune continued contemplating how he could help these desperate people. He realized that they would need at least 20 days to travel through the Soviet Union, and another 30 days to stay in Ja-

Visas for Life

pan. A total of 50 days would be necessary to enable the refugees to procure visas and travel to a third country.

Chiune sent a second cable. It detailed how, if given the time, it would be possible to help the refugees. But once again, he was denied permission, on the grounds that the Japanese Department of the Interior felt that such an action would endanger public security. The shipping company that operated the ferryboats between Vladivostok and the port city of Tsuruga, also rejected his request. They thought that such an action would compromise passenger safety.

As the situation became more intense, it began to affect my physical well-being. Due to lack of sleep and constant anxiety, I was unable to continue breast-feeding my third son, Haruki. To compound the problem, Haruki rejected milk from the bottle. We eventually ran out of milk. We still could not get out of the consulate to purchase anything. I tried to humor Haruki in the hall so that his crying would not distract my husband. Chiune was faced with, perhaps, the most important decision of his life.

By this time, the other consulates in Kaunas had been forced to close. After the Soviet-German Nonaggression Pact was signed on August 23, 1940, that same day the Soviet Union formally annexed Lithuania. The Japanese Consulate received instructions from the Soviets to close its doors and leave immediately. We were instructed by the Foreign Office to evacuate quickly.

The pressures were being felt to make our move as quickly as possible. Chiune was keenly aware that the Russians were closely monitoring his every move, and that they probably had been keeping a voluminous dossier on all of his recent and past activities. He knew that they considered him a high security risk, as Chiune was one of the few experts on the Soviet Union in the Japanese Foreign Ministry.

This element of imminent danger made our situation even more desperate as we prepared to leave Kaunas. I am sure that as these events unfolded, Chiune wished that he could turn back the clock. I'm sure he wished he had not brought his family into this dangerous assignment. When he was first told of this posting, he contemplated leaving without the family. However, I insisted that the family always stay together. There was now no doubt in my mind that we had done the right thing. We would face this critical situation together, as a family.

In a last desperate attempt, Chiune sent a third cable requesting permission to issue visas. Chiune was now going through periods of doubt and indecision. He vacillated from one position to another. He would think out loud and try to convince himself into being prudent and practical for the sake of the family. He would then remember the desperation of the people waiting outside.

At one point we discussed the possibility of leaving immediately, abandoning the entire situation, leaving it to the whims of fate. I quickly disagreed and said, "no, we cannot, it would be impossible for us to leave them." As I said this, a sense of relief came upon Chiune's face and I saw his familiar gentle smile. Then he said, "you're right. I will issue visas in defiance of the Foreign Ministry under my own authority as a Consul. He asked for my approval as he said, "I don't know what will happen to us, though." But I could only think of the thousands of lives who were depending on us at that moment. We could not escape this situation knowing so many lives were in danger. On this, Chiune and I were one. When I saw his beautiful smile, I felt at ease for a while.

When he received the third reply, it read, "the Foreign Ministry is opposed to hundreds of foreigners passing through Japan for reasons of public security." With this last reply, Chiune was now fully resolved to issue the visas.

Again, he asked for my approval, and I answered, "please do this!" Our minds worked together; we both knew that thousands of lives depended on our decision.

The family unanimously agreed to disobey the government's orders and issue the visas. Everyone, including Setsuko, agreed that we would put concern for ourselves aside and think about the people outside our gates. It was frightening. We worried for our lives, our future, Chiune's job, everything. But we prepared ourselves to face an uncertain future.

Chiune explained that if he went through with this decision to sign all the visas, he must be prepared to be dismissed by the Foreign Ministry. He also realized that in acting against his own government, he would lose all chance of advancement or be dismissed for violating public service regulations of the civil authorities. He reassured himself by thinking that should these events become reality, he still would be able to find employment using his Russian language skills. "I think I can make money with my Russian if I need to," he said, as if muttering to himself.

Chiune felt fairly sure that the Nazis would not harm his family, but he himself was prepared to give up his life. Now that he had come to this monumental decision, a feeling of relief came over him. This was characteristic of my husband. He always acted on his own beliefs and had the courage to listen to his moral convictions despite all outside pressures.

As I reflected on my husband, I thought about the young Chiune who followed his conviction to become a teacher rather than the doctor that his father wished him to be. Did he not endure hardships, because of this decision, to remain in school? Was he not the young man who, while studying at Waseda University, responded to an advertisement looking for students to study abroad for the Foreign Ministry? As a result, Chiune found himself as a clerk for the Foreign Ministry in Harbin. Was this not the same man who, because of his linguistic abilities, found himself teaching Russian at Harbin Gakuin (National University)? Was this not the same man who found himself, by the age of 32, working for the Japanese Embassy in Harbin, becoming known as one of the foremost authorities on Russia?

This was also the man who was asked to work for the Foreign Ministry of Manchukuo in 1932 as section chief of Russia, and was to become a key figure in the negotiations to acquire the North Manchurian Railroad from the Soviet Union. This purchase was one of the most significant accomplishments by Japan during this period. This was the man who eventually became Vice Chief of the Foreign Ministry of Manchukuo, but who suddenly resigned his post to return to Japan. His resignation was due to his abhorrence of the Japanese Military's cruel and inhuman treatment of their Chinese captives during the occupation of Manchuria. Once again, when faced with a moral dilemma, he chose to follow his strong moral convictions. Once again, these decisions based on humanitarianism, became instrumental in determining his fate. This became the pattern which he followed throughout his life.

Chiune talked about the situation outside our window. He said, "I have to do something. A young man comes into my home for protection. Is he dangerous? No. Is he a spy? No. Is he a traitor? No. He's just a Jewish teenager who wants to live." The choice was clear to Chiune. "I may have to disobey my government, but if I don't, I will be disobeying God."

We decided to issue the visas even though it meant risking his career and our lives. We both knew that we had to save these people. There was simply no choice in the matter. My husband and I never, for a single moment, doubted that we would take less than the necessary actions. We never regretted our decision.

Early the next morning, Chiune visited the Soviet Embassy. It was necessary that he get permission from the Soviets to let the Jews pass through Russia. Chiune was very persuasive with the Soviet officials. There was no other way to get to Japan. Without these transit visas, his visas would be of no use. I was concerned about his safe return from the Soviet Consulate because this was the first time he was going there himself, and I also knew that the Russians perceived him as a high security risk. Finally, after what seemed like a long time, he returned, his face glowing with happiness. The negotiations with the Russians had gone well. They were impressed with his command of the Russian language and said, "we can't tell the difference between your Russian and a native's." Because of his ability to clearly explain the situation, it was possible to have a frank and thorough discussion with the Soviets. As a result, Chiune was successful in completing negotiations for the Soviets to issue transit permits. Another factor that also helped the Soviets to be more cooperative was an economic factor or motivation. As it was learned, the Russians charged more than double fare to the Jewish refugees to ride the trains across Siberia and again to go across by boat from Vladivostok to Tsuruga.

Chiune explained that after he had put forth his request, the Soviet Consul had thought about it for a minute, looked at Chiune, and simply said, "okay, go ahead." That was it. I knew at that moment that we would help the refugees escape the Nazis.

Visas for Life

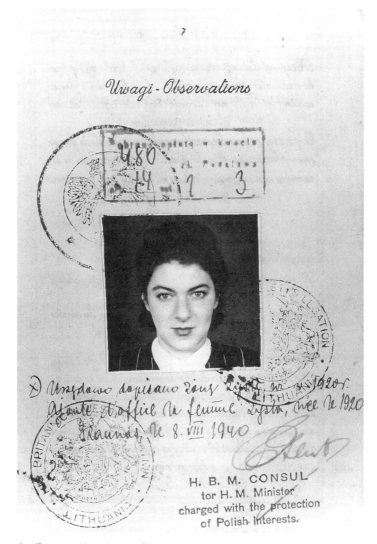

Sugihara survivor Susan Blumen on passport.

Issuing the Visas

By early dawn, there were many people anxiously waiting in front of the consulate. They wore coats to keep warm in the morning chill. Chiune announced his decision outside the consulate. "I'll issue visas to each and every one of you to the last," he said to the refugees. "So please wait patiently."

There was a momentary silence followed by an electricity that flowed through the crowd. People began rejoicing as they hugged and kissed one another. Others looked up and reached toward the sky in silent exaltation. Mothers picked up their children to share the joy with them. The magic of the moment filled me with gladness.

Chiune decided to open the garage door instead of the gate. At that point dozens of desperate people tried to scramble in. The crowd began to lose control and pandemonium began to take over.

"Please come in one by one," my husband shouted. Chiune devised a system that gave each person a number as they waited their turn in line. Borislav provided number cards to prevent a riot.

After drinking a cup of coffee, Chiune began what was to become an arduous task that would last for about one month. The procedure required to issue the visas was very time-consuming. Certain necessary steps had to be followed.

Chiune had to ascertain certain things. He had to determine if individuals had port-of-entry permits for the country of their destination, or the means of getting the funds to continue their journey. The primary problem was that he was the only one with the authority to issue these visas. No one could help him.

Because the Japanese Consulate in Kaunas was designed primarily to obtain international information, appropriate visa forms were scarce. This forced Chiune to record all the information by hand. He worked painstakingly to ensure that each name was printed correctly. Gudje, a German Lithuanian, who wanted to help save the Jews, worked hard alongside my husband. He helped stamp Chiune's name as Consul on the visas. In addition, some of the refugees helped him in the office. When Chiune handed visas to the applicants, he would look them in the eye and say, "Good luck." One survivor remembers him saying, "Vaya con Dios."

From the first day, Chiune never had time to stop for lunch. He skipped many other meals as well. Although lunch was prepared daily, Chiune did not eat. I was also too preoccupied to think about having lunch, and I had no inclination to eat lunch alone while Chiune continued to work.

Previously, the consulate opened at 9:00 a.m. and closed at

21

Visas for Life

5:00 p.m. Now Chiune worked from 8:00 a.m. into the late evening.

I would often stand on the stairs, straining my ears to hear something. Sometimes Chiune would stick his head out as I stood there. "How many people are left outside?" he'd shout up to me. The grounds were not visible from his office. "There are still many," I would tell him. In this way, Chiune provided me with a role in his work. This was a welcome relief from simply standing there watching.

My sister and I were concerned about his health because he had been working ceaselessly, skipping meals, and lacking sleep. His eyes were bloodshot from eye strain and lack of sleep. The fatigue showed deeply on his face. I was just 27 years old at the time and this ordeal was affecting me greatly. Fortunately, my sister was there to help care for the children, and her presence did much to reassure me.

Chiune's goal was to write out 300 visas a day. Due to circumstances such as lack of paper and ink, the need to handwrite everything, and the need for accuracy made it impossible to attain this goal. When we ran low on ink and could not go out to get more, we watered down the ink we still had. Again, Chiune's biggest problem was that he alone had the authority to issue the visas; he could not receive help.

For close to one month, Chiune sat unwavering for endless hours signing visas. From eight in the morning until late at night. Day after day for four weeks, he handwrote and signed the visas. Chiune wanted to write hundreds of visas a day, which normally would be more than one month's work for an entire consulate.

When people began climbing the fence to get into the compound, the staff had to go out and calm them down. Chiune reassured the people that as long as there was a single person left, he would not abandon them.

While writing the visas, Chiune unconsciously gripped his fountain pen so hard that it broke. This incident made it necessary for him to write in a cumbersome way with an old-fashioned pen and ink.

Since he was a strong man, Chiune was able to keep writing for almost an entire month. The strength of his body was a blessing. I worried about his hands and his physical energy, but he did not complain a bit. Chiune chose not to lose one

The People Who Escaped

In his office.

minute, because hundreds of people were standing in line in front of his consulate day and night, and they needed his help.

Each day's work left him drained and exhausted. Each visa was a lengthy document, comparable to writing two or three full paragraphs. After a long day, he went straight to bed. As he fell asleep, I massaged his arm, which was stiff and cramped from writing. Throughout this ordeal he continued his routine of rising early in the morning. Many people stood outside the consulate from morning until night waiting for visas. It was freezing at night, but many people slept in the adjacent park to ensure a spot near the front of the line. Chiune continued to write out visas with a determined resolve to issue as many visas as possible.

I offered to fill out the visas with Chiune, but he felt that this would be dangerous for me to do. If there was trouble, Chiune wanted to be solely responsible. I did not help with the visas. In fact, Chiune did not want me to come into the office at all during those four weeks. He did not want the family involved in any aspect of signing the visas.

One woman knelt down and kissed Chiune's feet when she received her visa. In gratitude, a businessman from Warsaw offered his technical knowledge and funds to Japanese companies. These gestures of appreciation inspired in Chiune a drive to continue issuing more visas.

Originally, Chiune numbered the visas and kept a list. Later he realized that would slow him down and reduce the total number of visas he could write. So he stopped numbering the visas and he also stopped charging the nominal fee. He also stopped interviewing the refugees. Chiune wanted to speed up the process in every possible way. He also worried that the Soviet occupation of Lithuania might prevent the exchange of Lithuanian currency into U.S. dollars. He wired the visa fees to the accounts section of the Foreign Ministry in Japan via the Lithuanian National Bank.

This routine continued for nearly a month. During that month, the Soviet government repeatedly insisted that Chiune leave Kaunas. My husband ignored these orders and continued issuing visas. Chiune also ignored orders from the Japanese Foreign Ministry, which were sent on August 2, to close and vacate the consulate. He continued issuing visas. He requested and received the Soviet Embassy's permission to remain in Kaunas until the end of August 1940.

Chiune was still in good health. He was able to maintain his stamina and dedication to issuing as many visas as possible. While his body remained strong, it was my husband's spirit that permitted him to continue working. However, about mid-August, Chiune came up to the first floor of the consulate and said, "I wonder if I should stop now?" Realizing that he was exhausted and felt dejection from prolonged fatigue, I encouraged him by saying, "many people are still waiting. Let's issue some more visas and save as many lives as we can." He nodded to me with a smile, appreciating my encouragement. According to the latest rumors, the Jews still remaining in Lithuania were in extreme danger of being killed. Again, Chiune's resolve to save as many lives as possible was further rekindled. My husband probably realized that if he were to quit now, he would regret it later.

There in the crowd
Waiting for visas
Is a boy
Clutching his father ever so tightly
His face is dirty

Jewish refugees in front of consulate gate.

Visas for Life

Soon after we left Kaunas, 10,000 Lithuanian Jews, one-third of the Jewish population of Kaunas, were rounded up, taken into the fort overlooking the hills of Kaunas, and shot by German murder squads. There were mass shootings for three days. These massacres were among the worst of the Holocaust. Before these massacres, 155,000 Jews lived in Lithuania, making up eight percent of the population. Many Lithuanian Jews requested and received my husband's visas. The Soviets, however, did not allow them to use these visas. The Lithuanian Jews were technically considered Soviet citizens. Unfortunately, most of these people were later killed. Years later, I learned that 94% of the Jews of Lithuania had been murdered.

Chiune continued issuing visas at the consulate until August 28. The Soviets were now pressuring us and demanding that we leave. When an urgent telegram came from the Japanese Foreign Ministry, demanding that Chiune close the consulate and leave immediately for Berlin, he realized that we really had to leave. The telegram read, "Lithuania is occupied by the Soviet Union. It is no longer an independent country."

Chiune continued issuing visas until the last minute, as he gave orders and instructions about locking the doors and packing our bags. As I was packing, I smelled something burning. The smoke was coming out of his basement office. In a panic, I screamed Chiune's name as I desperately pounded on his office door. He quickly appeared and said, "don't worry. I am just putting some papers in order." He was actually burning all of his confidential documents before the Soviets could confiscate them.

Time ran out. I will never forget the look of despair on the faces of the Jews who did not get visas as we left our consulate. Tears welled up in my eyes and I apologized to them in my mind as I asked for their forgiveness. Before continuing on our journey by train, we stayed in the center of town at the Hotel Metropolis in order to allow my exhausted husband some time to rest. Before we left the consulate, Chiune put up a notice on the gate telling people where we could be located. Many Jews came to the hotel, desperate for visas. Chiune continued to issue visas to the refugees from the hotel lobby.

Since Chiune had already sent all the necessary materials, such as, the seal of the Consul and other papers, to Berlin, he could no longer issue visas. Instead, he wrote out permission papers. I later learned that those who received these permission papers were also successful in their escape. This was probably due to the general state of confusion during wartime.

We stayed at the hotel until the end of August which was the deadline designated by the Soviets.

To the very last minute, Chiune continued issuing permission papers in the lobby. As he prepared to depart, he said, "please forgive me. I cannot write anymore. I wish you the best." Then, he bowed deeply to the people before him. They stood frozen before our eyes, as all hope faded from their faces.

We made our way to the train station. As our train pulled away, someone shouted, "Banzai, Nippon!" which means "Long live Japan!" One by one, a chorus of those words could be heard, "Banzai, Nippon!" When my husband issued visas, he asked recipients to say this. Always a diplomat, Chiune loved his homeland. Chiune felt that any appreciation felt by the refugees should be directed to his beloved country; not to him. He wanted the refugees to understand that he was merely an instrument, a diplomat, assigned to Lithuania by the country of Japan. Because of this, most of the refugees never had any idea how much Chiune risked issuing the visas. They thought he was acting with Japan's permission.

Chiune was giving the refugees advise by telling them to say "Banzai Nippon". He told them to use this phrase when they met immigration officials in Japan. He they would be more sympathetic.

When our train pulled away, we heard a man's voice crying out, "'Sempo' Sugihara, we will never forget you! We will see you again." Close to 30 years later, I would meet one of the people who shouted those words. This man, Yehoshua Nishri, would become a diplomat for the Israeli Foreign Ministry.

People started to run alongside the train. Chiune handed and threw blank visas out of the window. Later we heard that these visas were used to escape. People cried and ran along side of our train until we were out of sight.

"Father, are we going to go to Berlin?" Hiroki asked. My husband nodded quietly and closed his eyes. Chiune collapsed and fell asleep as the train pulled out of the station.

I was sad for the people left behind at the station without visas. I will not forget their eyes for the rest of my life.

Leaving Kaunas, on the train to Berlin.

The train pulls away,
Hands reaching out the window
Passing out visas
Hands reaching towards the windows
for visas for life —
HOPE

The transit visas were tickets to freedom and life for thousands of Jewish people. But these visas were only the beginning of a long and arduous journey for the Jewish refugees. From Lithuania, they traveled by the trans-Siberian railroad to the port of Vladivostok. There they boarded ships bound for Kobe, Japan. They spent a few months in Kobe. From there, most people were sent by Japan to Shanghai, where they spent the remainder of the war under the protection of the Japanese government. A few lucky refugees were able to immigrate to the United States, Canada, England, Argentina, Brazil, Australia, and Palestine. After the war, the refugees in Shanghai emigrated to various countries around the world.

Yukiko and Chiune (on right) at picnic in Japan, 1935.

Chapter 2

Life in Europe

Our First Meeting

THE FIRST MEETING between Chiune and I began with the question, "can you read this name?" I looked at the kanji characters Chiune had just written on his memo pad. "It could be Sempo, which sounds like the name of an artist, but if not, it could be Chiune," I said to this smiling man. My brother had brought him over to our home for dinner. As I answered, I wondered why he was asking me such a strange question, especially since this was our first meeting. He smiled. I liked art, and many Japanese artists at the time had similar names, such as Geppo, so I read it as 'Sempo.' My answer seemed to impress him as he replied, "You're the first

31

person who said 'Chiune.' It's not easy. Not many people can read it." Chiune was a very unusual and rare name. So went the first conversation between Chiune and I, the man I was to marry.

Since my father passed away, I had been living with my brother in Tokyo. After graduating from the university, my brother, Shizuo, worked for Nihon Insurance Company. In 1935, my brother visited the Foreign Ministry on business and met Chiune, who worked for the Foreign Ministry of Manchukuo (Manchuria). They became good friends and my brother invited Chiune for dinner. I learned about the key role that Chiune played in Japan's negotiations in the purchase of the Northern Manchurian Railroad. I also learned about Chiune's idealistic humanitarian principals. He seemed to live by these principles when he explained to me why he resigned his post as Foreign Minister of Manchukuo.

Since our first memorable meeting, Chiune began visiting our home two or three times a week. I began to get to know this very attractive and kind person. I dicovered many unusual and interesting facts about his past.

I learned that Chiune was born on January 1, 1900. He was born in the town of Yaotsu, in the Gifu Prefecture, 30 miles northeast of Nagoya. He was the second son in a middle-class Samurai family. Chiune had five brothers and one sister. Chiune's mother's maiden name was Yatsu Iwai. She was a very gentle woman. Chiune resembled his mother both in temperament and physical appearance. His father, Yoshimizu Sugihara, always wanted Chiune to become a doctor, but Chiune had his own ideas.

Chiune hoped to become an English teacher, and earned very good grades in English. By the time Chiune graduated high school, at the top of his class, he knew he wanted to live abroad and study literature. He had disappointed his father by intentionally failing the examination to get into medical school. He left the exam without filling out a single question. Chiune wanted to become a language teacher.

Chiune told me, "Since I had left my home against my father's wishes, I didn't receive any allowance from him. Sometimes my mother gave me some money secretly, but it wasn't enough to live on. So I had several part-time jobs," Chiune told me. Chiune had a very difficult time supporting

Life In Europe

Chiune's family, 1920. Father, four brothers and a sister.

himself in college. He held several positions. He was a news paper delivery man, longshoreman, and tutor.

"Why did you decide to work for the Foreign Ministry?" I asked. Chiune told me a little of his history. "Actually, I wanted to become an English teacher, but my father ordered me to become a doctor. I didn't want to be a doctor, so I left home in Korea and came back to Japan. Chiune explained, "Because of my father's business there, I was in Korea up until the end of my middle school. After I graduated from the Japanese Fifth Nagoya High School, which is now called Zuryo

Chiune's mother, Yatsu Sugihara (left).

High School (in Korea), I went to Tokyo and entered Waseda University."

Every time I'd ask him something unexpected, Chiune would smile, look directly at me, and answer my spontaneous questions sincerely. It seemed strange to me that he addressed me in such a sincere way. In those days, men did not often listen to women. They did not take women seriously in conversation or ask them serious questions. There was no one like Chiune. He was not chatty, but it was clear that he was trying to have a real conversation with me. He wasn't trying to talk at me, but with me.

One day, in 1919, Chiune saw an advertisement by the Foreign Ministry in the classified section of a government newspaper. The Foreign Ministry was looking for people who wanted to study abroad and might be interested in a diplomatic career. Chiune took the newspaper and hurried down to the Foreign Ministry.

The person in charge told him, "You may be better off learning Russian rather than English now, because we are not recruiting English speakers this year." For this reason, Chiune decided to learn Russian. He took and passed his English examination. He started learning Russian as soon as he arrived in his new home in Harbin, China. Chiune was sent by the Japanese Foreign Ministry to Harbin Gakuin, where he studied Russian. He was only 19 years old.

Many years later, I heard that Chiune was known as an eccentric person among his friends, and that everyone thought he had a unique sense of humor. Each morning when he went to school, he tied a pen and a tiny ink bottle on each end of a string. He looped this string around his ear. Even though his friends laughed at him, he would say, "with this pen and ink I can take notes anywhere I go." This was silly because I heard that he never took notes while he was in his class. He had a photographic memory. While Chiune was studying Russian, he would carry a dictionary in his pocket, and when he finished memorizing a page, he would tear it up and throw it away. He memorized every word in the Russian dictionary. I think he was able to master Russian quickly because of his natural gift for languages and his power of concentration. By the end of the Second World War, Chiune spoke Russian, English, German, French, Chinese, and of course, Japanese.

While studying at Harbin Gakuin, Chiune stayed with a White Russian family. There were many White Russians in Harbin and it was common for students at the University to stay in their homes. The cosmopolitan nature of Harbin opened Chiune's eyes to the diversity and excitement of the world. He graduated with honors. At the same time, he also adopted the Greek Orthodox Christian religion.

With his linguistic talent, Chiune was hired as a clerk and interpreter in the Ministry of Foreign Affairs. He also was asked to teach at Harbin Gakuin one year after he graduated. It was extraordinary to be hired as a teacher so soon after graduating. He taught there part-time for three years, until he was 32 years old. The Japanese language school had a motto, "do much for others, and expect little in return." This motto would affect Chiune for the rest of his life.

When Chiune talked, he always smiled, except when he talked about his mother's death. He told me, "I was drafted and served one year in the Japanese army. While serving in the military, I received a telegram that told me that my mother had passed away. " He couldn't stop the tears from running down his face. His army instructor scolded him. He was so upset about her death that he couldn't run holding his rifle. The tears glistened in his eyes as he reminisced about his mother.

Chiune's next assignment was serving in the Japanese military occupation government of Manchuria, China. In March 1932, Japan occupied part of northern China and called it Manchukuo. Chiune was asked to work for the Foreign Ministry of the Manchukuo Occupation Government. He became the head of the North Manchurian Mission Office. He was later promoted to Vice Minister of the Foreign Affairs Department. He was next in line to become the Minister of Foreign Affairs in Manchuria.

Chiune's job was mainly to negotiate with the Soviet Consul in Harbin or in Dairen. Mr. Slavki was the Soviet Consul at that time and he later became the Soviet Ambassador to Japan. When Chiune met Soviet people, he'd introduce himself to them half jokingly and say, "my name is Pavlo Sergeivich Sugihara." He used a Russian name that was close to Sempo. People said that such witty remarks pleased the Russians.

He left for his new post as Section Chief of the Soviet Union, and negotiated the purchasing of the Northern Man-

Life In Europe

Chiune Sugihara, 1920.

churian Railroad from the Soviet Union. This saved the Japanese government millions of dollars, and infuriated the Soviets. As a result, the Soviet government became quite wary of Chiune, and he was not allowed back into Russia for a long time.

To assess the value of the railroad, Chiune had the help of a few hundred Chinese and Koreans, whom he had helped ear-

Chiune was a reserve lieutenant in the army, 1920 (middle row, second from left).

lier. Chiune had made many Chinese and Korean friends because he was the only government employee who had been willing to help them when their region was devastated by a flood. He had gone from village to village, and helped people estimate their damages in order to rebuild. This activity was not encouraged by the Japanese government, but Chiune helped them anyway. Later, when negotiations regarding the railroad began with the Soviets, these Chinese and Koreans friends proved to be quite an asset. Their information and research ultimately saved the Japanese government millions of dollars.

After a few years Chiune became the Vice Chief of the Foreign Ministry of Manchukuo. Suddenly he resigned his post and returned to Japan just short of obtaining the position of Minister of Foreign Affairs of Manchukuo. Chiune resigned from his position because he was greatly disturbed by his government's policy in China and their cruel treatment of the Chinese people. He resigned his post in protest in 1934.

We met in 1935 when Chiune returned to Japan. When I asked him why he had resigned his post in the Foreign Ministry of Manchukuo, he said, "The Japanese dealt cruelly with the Chinese. They didn't consider them human. I couldn't bear that," he quietly explained. Upon returning from Harbin, Chiune worked once again for the Foreign Ministry in Japan.

Now that you have heard a little bit about Chiune, I would like to write a few words about myself.

I was born Yukiko Kikuchi on December 17, 1913 in Numazu. I am the first daughter of a middle-class family. My mother's name was Tsuru Kikuchi, and my father, who was a teacher, was named Fumio Kikuchi. My hometown is Tohno which is in the Iwate Prefecture. It is very cold there, and has a traditional, conservative atmosphere.

My family was very close. We have never had a fight, not even among siblings. My parents were always very sweet. I never quarreled with anybody. I was a little dreamer, scared of nothing in the world.

Because my father was a teacher, we moved from Morioka to Mito. Later we moved again to Shikoku. My father was the principal of the Shido Business High School and we lived in the heart of Shikoku. My father was considered a great principal because he was an innovative educator. He forbid the school from expelling students.

Meanwhile, I dreamed of becoming a poet and an artist. When I was five years old, I already made up poems. I should not use the word "poem," because for somebody that young to really be able to write a poem is unusual. I really liked the sound of words. I was impressed with their beauty and the power of their meanings and subtle differences. I especially liked creating my own nursery rhymes.

After I graduated from high school, I started to write poems for relaxation. I contributed them to some magazines. After some of my poems were published, I became more and more enthusiastic about poetry. Then, I shifted entirely away from composing regular poetry to writing *tanka*. I especially enjoyed art and thought about becoming an artist or going to Paris to become a beauty specialist.

My personality was one which made me want to try many things. My mother was a woman who was ahead of her times. She bought a watch and a pair of high heel shoes as soon as they started selling them in Japan.

People would ask me, "what kind of man do you want to marry?" I'd say, "I don't want to marry." I want to be an independent woman and I don't want to depend on a man." I thought that the young men of that day were not reliable. Even if I did marry I could not settle for an arranged marriage, which was common in Japan. I always knew that my life would be different than that of most Japanese women.

Chiune later told me, he liked me instantly when we first met. He liked me, he said, because I reminded him of a Russian girl he had liked a long time ago. I also felt the same about him. Soon, he became a part of our family. He listened

Yukiko as a baby with her mother, Tsuru Kikuchi, and brother, Shizuo.

Life In Europe

Bound for Finland via United States, 1937.

to me and he was interested in what I had to say.

One day, he asked me hesitantly, "will you marry me? Will you marry me, please?" I had never seen him look so serious. I was 21 years old. "Why do you want to marry me?" I asked. "Because you are a person that can adjust well to living in a foreign country and would be an ideal wife of a diplomat," he replied.

At that time, a marriage for love was not easily permitted. Marriages based on love were uncommon at that time. Chiune was 13 years older than I, and I thought that a marriage with an older man might provide more security for my future than a marriage with a young man. I made my decision right at that moment. "If you think of me in such a way, I will accept," I said. We agreed to marry. A smile spread across Chiune's face.

As Chiune was a Greek Orthodox Christian, I consented to be baptized when I married him. I am not a very religious person, but now I consider myself a member of the Greek Orthodox church. I was given the Christian name of Maria. We were married on February 1935 in Tokyo.

In 1937, we were posted to the Japanese diplomatic office in Helsinki, Finland. From Finland, Chiune and I were originally assigned to Turkey. At the last minute the Japanese government decided to send Chiune to Lithuania to open a one-person consulate. There was perhaps more activity on the Lithuanian border than in Turkey. Consequently, the Japanese

Foreign Ministry felt that they needed Chiune in Lithuania to report on Soviet and German war plans.

Since he spoke Russian fluently, he had confidence that this skill would help him find a good job. As a diplomat, Chiune's dream was to become the Japanese Ambassador to the Soviet Union. He believed he could make a difference in Japan's future serving in Russia.

The Departure

After Chiune and I were married, we settled in Ikebukuro, Tokyo. Chiune had formed friendships with many of the Russians who had escaped the Russian Revolution and who lived in Japan. My husband's friends would sometimes visit us. It was the first time that I had heard Russian. I couldn't understand what Chiune and his friends were saying, but fortunately, I started to learn some basic Russian by listening to them.

Chuine's colleagues from the Foreign Ministry didn't visit us often. They did come for special occasions like New Year's Day. The other exception was that most of the ministry wives from my husband's section met regularly at a Japanese-style restaurant. There were about ten of us, and we sat from the head of the table down, depending on our husbands' positions. Most of the women had previously lived in foreign countries. Their conversations were mainly about their overseas travels.

At that time, the sections of the Foreign Ministry were separated by language. There were not many people in the Russian Section. I felt that there was some competition between the wives. I heard that the women who were stationed in Moscow were separated into two groups and were fighting amongst themselves. I thought such behavior was intolerable, and tried to remain uninvolved.

Right after Chiune and I got married, we heard about the *2.26 Incident*. This was an attempted coup d'état by some young radicals to overthrow the current Japanese government. The *2.26 Incident* refers to the date of February 26. This attempt had failed, but as the Manchurian conflict escalated, my husband left immediately to go to his office. It had been snow-

Life In Europe

ing hard for two days, and now Tokyo was under martial law. I phoned Chiune at the office, but I couldn't reach him. By midnight, he still hadn't returned, and I stayed up all night worrying. I didn't hear from him until the next day.

After the *2.26 Incident*, Japan had become almost entirely controlled by the Army. My husband was very upset. He did not agree with the imposition of martial law. Soon after this, I discovered that I was expecting a child. Chiune held my hands as I told him the news. He loved children and he used to tell me, "let's have a child soon."

In November 1936, the Japan-Germany Anti-Comintern pact was signed. It seemed to both of us that the world was

Visas for Life

advancing toward war.

Chiune and I were talking about how we could feel our baby moving. My husband and I were happy. In September 1936, our first son, Hiroki, was born. My husband was in Kamchatka, Russia, as an interpreter for the negotiation of a Japanese-Soviet Fishing agreement. When he came back to Japan, he rushed into the house and picked up Hiroki, who was sleeping next to me. He said to him, "look at me! I'm your father!" He held newborn Hiroki clumsily, with hands that were not used to holding such a tiny baby.

Six months after Hiroki was born, my husband said, "the Foreign Ministry has decided that we will leave soon for my new post in the Soviet Union." We were supposed to go overseas for two years.

My younger sister, Setsuko, who lived with us at that time, decided to go with us. She wanted to help as well as to study. Happily, I started packing. Before we finished packing, Chiune told me that there was a problem. He said that the Soviet

Hiroki and Chiune, Helsinki, 1938.

Life In Europe

Union didn't want to issue him a visa. The Soviets were still disturbed about the Northern Manchurian Railroad negotiations that occurred in 1934.

The Foreign Ministry decided instead to send my husband to the Japanese Embassy in Helsinki, Finland. It was September 1937. While it was fastest to travel to Helsinki through the Soviet Union, Chiune was not permitted travel there. We had to go to Helsinki via the United States.

We went by ship because airplane travel was virtually nonexistent. The trip with our one-year-old Hiroki started. Several days after we left Japan, we entered the port in Seattle and traveled over land to New York. Since we were on a tight schedule, we didn't have the chance to go sightseeing.

When we arrived in New York, someone from the Japanese Foreign Ministry was waiting for us. As soon as he saw us, he said, "you need to get on the ship right now." We didn't even have time to say hello before he said this. We were supposed to stay one night in New York, but our itinerary hadn't considered the time difference between New York and Japan. We hurried to the dock. There, I saw a big white building in the distance, but no ships. "Where is our ship?" I asked. Our host pointed and said, "that's it." The white building was actually a 40,000 ton ship anchored offshore. This beautiful German ship, named the "Bremen," was a famous passenger ship on which wealthy Americans and Germans traveled. It had a pool and a movie theater. Plump, middle-aged women sunbathed on the deck during the day, and in the evening, they dressed up, adorned in gorgeous jewelry. We had three meals a day in the dining room. We had to change our clothes for every meal. Since I didn't have many dresses or pieces of jewelry, I spent most of the time in my *kimonos*. It takes a lot of time to get into a *kimono*. Having to change three times a day made my time on the Bremen anything but relaxing.

It took us four days to reach Port Bremenhaven in Germany. We finally arrived in Helsinki by train via Holland and Switzerland.

The Country of the Midnight Sun

There were many lakes in Helsinki, and the Minister's home

was in a building facing one of them. Chiune worked under Minister Sako as the first official interpreter. Minister Sako had left his wife in Japan and was stationed in Helsinki by himself. Since a diplomat had to take a partner to parties or ceremonies, Minister Sako asked me to accompany him in place of his wife.

Minister Sako invited us to live with him, and we accepted his invitation. Sako liked to party and drink, so we drank with him almost every night. He drank Japanese sake and he had a bottle of whiskey waiting for us every night. Then he would say, "you can't go to bed until you finish drinking this." So Chiune and I ended up finishing a bottle of whiskey every night. But shortly after Chiune started working in Helsinki, Minister Sako left for his new post in Poland. My husband became the Acting Minister.

This was my first overseas experience and I was only 24 years old. My role as wife of the Acting Minister was quite a big responsibility. First of all, languages were a problem. I had learned English at school, but I couldn't speak it very well. If I couldn't communicate with people when I attended formal receptions with my husband, I would not be effective as a diplomat's wife. I studied French and German everyday. Many people did not speak English in Europe at that time. French was the spoken language of diplomatic society, but German was spoken almost everywhere we went by the many Germans who lived in Finland. The diplomats I met in Europe spoke many different languages; one spoke sixteen. I decided to use German most of the time. I took dance and etiquette lessons in addition to my language lessons.

My first formal invitation in Finland was to a reception given by the Swedish Minister. Since I liked purple, I attended the reception wearing a purple dress.

Wearing a veil of violet.
I accompany my husband,
To an evening gala
At the Swedish Legation

Everyday we hosted, or were invited to, many dinner parties, evening parties, and tea parties. The residence in Helsinki was very big, and we often invited over 100 guests. People enjoyed

Chiaki and Chiune.

talking until dinner started. After dinner we danced. The employees knew when to serve alcohol and when to start serving dinner. In Europe, there were specialists to handle these events and we could leave everything to them.

At the dinner parties, each Ambassador's wife wore an

evening dress with jewelry that had been passed down from generation to generation. I made myself an evening dress. Japanese women look beautiful in their *kimonos,* so most of the Japanese diplomats' wives wore them. People would constantly come up to me and touch the sleeves of my kimono, remarking, "I've never seen such beautiful silk." Silk was expensive in Europe, and a *kimono* attracted a lot of attention. They didn't understand the function of the decorative sash, the *obi,*. The *obi* seemed mysterious to Europeans. A person looking at the back of my *obi* would ask me, "do you put a baby here?"

Women were often asked to dance after dinner. To refuse was considered rude. I was always wearing a *kimono,* which was not easy to dance in. The Europeans were tall with long legs, and being smaller, I became tired following their movements. I also had trouble with my sandals, my *zori,* when I was dancing.

When we invited guests for dinner, we usually served French cuisine. We hired a Finnish cook when we had guests. There were some Japanese cooks at the Legation. We would eat Japanese food when we didn't have guests or when we only invited other Japanese. Once a year, we had a meeting for the local Japanese delegates. We once hosted a party of skiers from Japan. It was our job to take care of visitors from the Japanese government. Finland was pro-Japanese, and there was a Japanese-Finnish Association. We exchanged many aspects of our respective cultures.

I attended dinner parties or evening parties in *kimonos,* but I attended tea parties during the day in Western clothing. I had to order new clothes from my tailor for each party. If I had a new outfit made, I had to get a bag, a hat, and a pair of shoes to match. It took time, but I gradually became used to the busy life of a diplomat's wife.

We would always travel in a car with the Japanese flag on it. The first time I went shopping by car, I got out by myself, holding my own shopping bags. The driver quickly explained that he would always have to accompany me. I couldn't even go window shopping by myself. Since we had to be dressed up all day long, even in our homes, an additional clothing allowance was provided for the wives of Ambassadors and Ministers. The formality of our lives was a pressure for me. I felt as

Life In Europe

Japanese Embassy Party, Helsinki, 1938.

if there was no breathing room or freedom.

Although there was a Japanese Legation in Helsinki, no one really knew about Japan. I was often asked if I was Chinese when I went into the shops. People sometimes made funny remarks, such as, "you are Japanese, but you are not yellow." I was perplexed when people would say, "I've heard that men and women bathe together in Japan." Such questions and comments made me realize the lack of understanding about Japan that existed in Finland.

Our lives were busy, but on Sundays, we would relax by taking the family for a drive. My husband started learning to drive after we arrived in Helsinki. Our driver used to be the school master at a driving school, so Chiune decided to learn from him. Several days after Chiune received his license, the driver came to me in the middle of the night saying that our car had been stolen. I was about to wake up my husband, when I realized he wasn't there. A few hours later, I heard the car and saw Chiune get out of it with a look of satisfaction on his face. Though he had just gotten his driver's license, he usually had to sit quietly in the car while the driver chauffeured him. Chiune, who really wanted to drive by himself, drove secretly at night. It was a characteristic of his personality to always do what he wanted.

Visas for Life

The opera was another pleasure for us in Helsinki. Once we had invited a singer, who had played Madame Butterfly, to the Legation for dinner. She was half Japanese and half Italian. She performed nothing but the opera "Madame Butterfly." I believe that she had never visited Japan.

Once we visited the classical music conductor and composer, Sibelius, who had the impressive chiseled look of a sculpture. He autographed his portrait and gave it to us with his record, "Finlandia."

In winter, thick ice formed on the lake and we saw people walking across it to an island in the middle. The sound of the bell from the church on the island would come over the ice like silver. The winters were harsh, but the beauty of winter in Northern Europe was very special.

Summer nights in Helsinki were light, and summer was a time when diplomats could take vacations and relax. We rented a cottage in the country and enjoyed the time to ourselves. There was a white birch forest around the cottage and we could hear the sound of squirrels climbing up and down the trees. During the white nights, the sky was blue. Our cottage didn't have any blinds and the light came into our room through the curtains. I used to walk to the lake near our cottage when I couldn't sleep. Though it was summer, it was cold because we were in a northern country. The fresh air surrounding me was comfortable. The quiet made me feel as though I were part of the moonlight.

The following year, 1938, our second son, Chiaki, was born. I was only thinking of girl's names because I wanted a girl. I was a little surprised that I had a boy. Chiune did not have a preference. He looked critically on the traditional Japanese custom in which boys were treasured more than girls. His idea toward the children was, "whether they are a girl or a boy, we have to bring them up the same." He loved our children and never scolded them. When our boys misbehaved and troubled people, I would ask him to scold them, but he never did.

By March 1938, Germany had advanced into the Rhineland, and anti-Semitism was getting worse in Germany. The Berlin-Rome Axis was signed in October of that year. The war was drawing near. A tense atmosphere existed in most of Europe, but we still had a quiet life.

Spies sometimes visited the Japanese and other Legations in Helsinki. After the war, I learned that Mr. Izumi, who was the second secretary of the Legation, was a double agent. His wife was a White Russian, and my husband's friend. She often visited the Legation and then disappear. My sister and I also thought that she might be a spy. "Where is your wife?" I asked Mr. Izumi. He would respond, "she is traveling in Switzerland." Mr. Izumi was a clever spy, probably greater than the notorious Soviet spy, Sorge.

In March 1939, Germany annexed Bohemia and Moravia. In April, Italy annexed Albania. A military alliance was formed between Germany and Italy. In August, the German-Soviet Nonaggression Pact was signed. This would lead to the beginning of the war that would involve all of Europe. With these events came the sudden order for my husband to be transferred to a one-person Japanese Consulate in Kaunas, Lithuania.

Japanese Consulate, Königsberg, Germany, 1941.

Chapter 3:

The Dark Cloud

Berlin

AFTER KAUNAS we went to Berlin. When we were leaving Kaunas, Chiune left a note instructing refugees who could not get visas to go to the Japanese Embassy in Moscow to try to get visas. We later learned that this recommendation did help a few people acquire visas.

When we arrived in Berlin, Chiune immediately went to report to Saburo Kurusu, who had replaced Ambassador Hiroshi Oshima, to receive further instructions. Former Ambassador Oshima had just been called back to Tokyo in December 1939, but was scheduled to return in December 1940. Ambassador Oshima, an army general, was pro-German, whereas Saburo

Visas for Life

Brandenberg Gate, Berlin, 1940.

Kurusu was pro-American and pro-English.

During his meeting with Ambassador Kurusu, no accusations or questions were brought up about Chiune's issuing visas in Kaunas. This could have been because of the turmoil that was taking place throughout Europe.

The Soviet Union crushed Finland in March 1940. In June, the French surrendered to Germany. In September, the German airforce started their bombing raids on England. The Axis

Tripartite Pact was signed on September 27. That spring, U-Boats and British merchant ships had begun the Battle of the Atlantic, and Hitler invaded and conquered Denmark and Norway. Hitler set in motion the Holocaust when, on October 16, 400,000 Jews were herded into the Warsaw Ghetto.

We think that due to all of these events in Europe, what happened in Kaunas was overlooked. At that time, the Japanese Army controlled the Japanese government, including the diplomatic service. Another reason that could have delayed an immediate confrontation regarding Chiune's visas, may have been that he held the military rank of Lieutenant. The army had given their approval that he be appointed Japanese Consul in Lithuania. The army was also aware that Chiune was a strong proponent of peace. They knew Chiune advocated utilizing peaceful measures, rather than resorting to aggressive ones to solve problems between nations. I personally believe that the army and the foreign ministry chose, for the time being, to ignore Chiune's opposition of its orders. The army's need for his contributions as Consul far surpassed the need to take disciplinary action against him.

At the same time, in 1939, two important movements were forming in Japan. The more popular movement was one advocating an alliance with Germany. Another small movement, whose proposal was formulated secretly by a handful of powerful, Japanese diplomats and military officers. This proposal called for the establishment of a "free zone" for Jewish people fleeing Nazi persecution in Manchuria.

This plan had very strong economic and political overtones. The Japanese government was encouraged by the Nazis to institute an official policy of anti-Semitism against the Jews. The Japanese government refused to do so. In an internal memo, the Japanese government stated that the Japanese were victims of racism themselves, so why would Japan institute a racist policy against the Jewish people?

Matsuoka, the foreign minister of Japan who signed the Axis pact with Hitler on September 1940 said, "I first want to assure you that anti-semitism will never be adopted by Japan. True, I concluded a treaty with Hitler, but I never promised to be an anti-semite. And this is not only my personal opinion, but it is the principle of the entire Japanese empire."

Matsuoka added that if Germany ever demanded that Japan

persecute Jews, he would rather tear up the Axis alliance than to submit to such a demand.

As a result of this statement, over 30,000 Jews were allowed to live in relative peace in Hongkew, in the Japanese-controlled section of Shanghai, China. Many of these Jews had received Chiune's visas. Had Chiune been aware of this policy, his decision to sign the visas would have been much easier to make.

When I reflect back now, I am glad we were in Kaunas to help the Jews. I truly believe it was our fate to be there at the right time. If it had been one month later, they might have all been killed. I also truly believed that we were guided by a higher power.

An individual who played a role leading to Chiune's final decision was Lieutenant Makoto Onodera. He was a Japanese army attaché assigned to the Japanese Embassy in Sweden. Onodera did much to help the Jewish refugees. He was very sympathetic to their cause. Onodera who later worked hard to promote ending the war against the United States. Chiune continued to communicate with Onodera after we left Kaunas, and after the war.

The Stream of Moldau

Europe had changed a lot during the year we had spent in Lithuania. We were in Berlin temporarily, waiting for our next assignment. After we left Lithuania, I worried about what the Japanese Foreign Ministry would say to Chiune about the visas he had issued in Kaunas. My fears were diminished when Chiune came back from a visit with Ambassador Kurusu at the Japanese Embassy. Chiune told me, "Ambassador Kurusu did not say anything about the visas." His words swept away the dark cloud in my mind. Chiune then said, "We will soon be leaving for my new post in Prague." It was September 1940.

Consul General Ichige, in Prague, was leaving his post and returning to Japan because of personnel changes made by Foreign Minister Matsuoka. My husband was recommended for Ichige's position. Now, hurriedly, we had to move again. Even before we left for Chiune's new assignment in Prague, Nazi

The Dark Cloud

With a warm and winning personality, Sugihara, like Oscar Schindler, was able to manipulate policies for humanitarian ends.

Germany had informally demanded that all diplomats leave Czechoslovakia. Because of this, Chiune considered his new post a temporary one.

The Moldau River flowed through the center of Prague. The bells of St. Svatyvit, the magnificent cathedral, resounded throughout the city morning and evening. The rows of quiet, medieval-style houses and the elegant sculptures lining the seven bridges that crossed the river inspired me to paint them on canvas. When we moved to Prague, the preceding Consul General was still at the consulate, so our family stayed in a hotel until he left for Japan.

The consulate was a tall building facing the Moldau. Its interior walls were luxuriously covered with Japanese silk. One of the two rococo-style rooms was completely decorated in gold, and the other in silver. The silver room even had a silver piano. Its chandelier was made of Czechoslovakian crystal.

My husband and I went back to the life we knew before Kaunas. We were living the social life of a diplomat and his wife. Parties were once again held nightly. We lived with three officers, five maids, one cook, and a young Japanese girl who was studying art. I was nervous living in a war-zone, but when I compared it to our time in Kaunas, I felt better. The youngest maid, Marnya, was a friend to my children and she took good care of them.

I started studying German again, in a class at the consulate. In addition to the diplomatic corps, there were many exchange students around. About 50 Japanese students who were living in Prague attended the same class.

When the weather was pleasant, we went driving to the outskirts of Prague. We saw the ruins of structures built by the Bohemian Dynasty, which had prospered in medieval times. We also holiday trips to Rome, Venice, and Switzerland during this time.

On September 27, 1940, shortly after we had moved to Prague, Japan concluded the Triple Alliance with Germany and Italy. People in Prague were not familiar with Japan or its culture, and we did not feel the effects of the changes brought about by the Alliance. Hungary, Romania, and Czechoslovakia eventually entered into the Triple Alliance. By March 1941, Bulgaria had also joined. Germany relished its moment of glory. Hitler's army invaded Greece in April 1940. Germany was conquering Europe everywhere.

One day, the German Foreign Minister, Joachim von Ribbentrop, called a meeting of all the diplomats in Prague. When the German-Soviet Nonaggression Pact was concluded, von Ribbentrop signed the secret treaty to divide Poland and annex Lithuania. I heard von Ribbentrop was terrible.

When Chiune came home from the meeting he said, "I feel good today." He told me about events that had taken place at the meeting. A ferocious German shepherd was tied up at the entrance of the room, and the dog seemed to be waiting for its master's signal. When Chiune entered the room full of dignitaries, von Ribbentrop was sitting arrogantly at a big desk beneath a picture of Hitler.

Ribbentrop told the diplomats, "it is inconvenient for us that you are in Czechoslovakia. We would like you to leave immediately." He spoke in a commanding tone. The diplomats from different companies kept quiet because of his threatening and authoritative attitude. At this time the Nazis were at the peak of their strength. No one was brave enough to say

The Dark Cloud

anything to him, and von Ribbentrop understood this. The silence was suddenly broken by my husband. Chiune stood up, stared at von Ribbentrop, and inquired calmly, "you cannot just order us to leave. Would you please explain your reasons?" In the presence of my husband's assured and dignified attitude, Von Ribbentrop was left speechless

Not only was von Ribbentrop surprised by Chiune's confidence, but the other Nazi officials were also taken aback by what my husband said.

Chiune's response to von Ribbentrop asserted his representation of the Japanese government, a member of the Triple Alliance. Chiune's inquiry to Ribbentrop indirectly was a reminder to him that Japan was an equal partner in the alliance and not a subordinate one. I felt exhilarated hearing about this episode from Chiune.

While we lived in Prague, my husband compiled his documents from Kaunas. He began doing so because the Japanese Foreign Ministry ordered all of its diplomats to report the number of visas they had issued. According to his report on February 28, 1941, Chiune had issued a total of 1,092 visas between July 27 and August 31, 1940. However, he stopped numbering in early August, so I think he actually issued more than that. (editors note: In 1994, Boston University professor Hillel Levine discovered a list of visa recipients in the Daimyo Archives in Tokyo with 2,193 names on it. Scholars believe that one visa was good for an entire family, and since many of the refugees had been with their children, the number of Jews who escaped through Japan with Sugihara visas was probably more than 6,000. Some historians and eyewitnesses believe the number of people Chiune saved might be as high as 10,000. Included in the list were 300 students and faculty of the Mir Yeshiva, which was a large Jewish religious academy. It was the only Jewish Yeshiva saved in its entirety from the Holocaust.)

Our joyful life in Prague came to a close after six months. Ambassador Oshima, who had been residing in Berlin since December 1940, called for Chiune and asked him to come to Berlin. At the same time, the Nazis formally told the local diplomats had to leave. The order stated, "The general consulates in the protected territory of Bohemia-Moravia no longer have diplomatic privilege."

Ambassador Oshima was very friendly to my husband and told him, "I'm sorry that it's midwinter now and it will be a bother to you, but we depend on your Russian. We'd like to move you to Königsberg, Germany, near Russia, to open a consulate there. You can take some officers with you." He continued, "I'd like you to come back to visit me soon so we can have a drink together," he told Chiune.

On April 27, 1941, Germany defeated the allied forces of Greece and Yugoslavia, which were supported by Great Britain. This assault took Germany only 18 days, but it was said that Hitler's attempt to invade the Soviet Union was delayed for six months due to Germany's war with these smaller countries. Shortly before the invasion of the Soviet Union by Germany, the Nazis forced the diplomats of the Axis countries to leave Prague.

My husband's job as Consul General in Königsberg was to gather information for Japan. We traveled to Königsberg from Prague by car. On our way, we stopped at Pirzen, famous for its beer. We changed drivers at the border because our driver from Prague was not allowed to enter Germany. The German driver, who was waiting for us, took over and we continued up the mountains. The road was icy, and just as we arrived at the top of a mountain, the car spun around completely and we almost fell into the valley below. The driver probably wasn't used to our car, and he may have been blinded by the setting sun.

I remember a story I heard when we stopped at Potsdam, home of the splendid Sans S*ouci* palace of King Friedrich. Next to the palace, there was a windmill that emitted a loud noise when it rotated. The King ordered that the windmill be stopped. The old man who operated the windmill sued the King in a court in Berlin. He said, "to grind is my job; that is how I make my living. If I cannot use my windmill, I cannot live." The old man won. This story is known as the "The Windmill in Potsdam."

The Small Island That Surprised Europe

It was March 1941 when we moved to Königsberg, a small, quiet town in Germany. There was a school in Königsberg in which the philosopher Kant had studied. We rented a large two-story house through the municipal office and the Department of Protocol, and soon after, Chiune opened the consulate. The city authorities were told we were coming, and they were very cooperative. Seishiro Kuroda came from the Embassy in Berlin to help us settle in. The consulate had a large garden with many apple and pear trees. It resembled a fruit orchard, with squirrels playing in the trees.

"Give the squirrels some peanuts," I told Hiroki as I gave him some peanuts. Hiroki went out to the garden with his

Visas for Life

brothers, and right away the squirrels played on their shoulders. When we opened the windows in the morning, the squirrels would come into the house and beg for peanuts. The squirrels and the children became good friends.

A few days after we opened the consulate, about 30 members of the Hitler Youth came to greet us. When the children and I met them they called out, "Heil Hitler." They were young boys whose voices still hadn't changed. At that time, few people still said, "Guten Tag" (Good-day). "Heil Hitler" was the common greeting. Each family had a picture of Hitler in their house.

A child makes friends easily, and my children made many friends. The children had a good time doing things together, like camping out and going to birthday parties. My children would sometimes make friends with German soldiers, and bring them back to the consulate.

The American Consulate was still open in Königsberg. The air raids hadn't started yet, so we had a quiet life. We also continued the life of diplomats, but without the gala parties. Sometimes we invited guests for dinner. Until the United States entered the war, we invited their diplomats and families over for dinner.

I knew that the lives of most people were getting more and more complicated. While diplomats and their families had enough to eat, the local people needed ration coupons to obtain food, and could not easily get items such as coffee or vegetables. I planted vegetables in the garden and gave some to my neighbors. I also picked apples and pears from the trees with the children from the neighborhood. When I got coffee, I gave some to our neighbors, who were very thankful.

On May 5, 1941, I put up *koinobori*, Japanese carp kites symbolizing strength and courage, which I had brought from Japan for my boys; I invited the neighborhood mothers and children. The press came that day and were surprised to see our *koinobori*. We had a wonderful day. This was also a busy few days for Chiune. It was May 9 and Chiune had just sent a report to the Foreign Ministry in Japan about the movements of the Germans just before they invaded the Soviet Union. He reported that ten Nazi Army trains came to Königsberg from Berlin almost every day; about ten steamships, including a 30,000 ton ship, had been moored at Pilau Port; and a large

The Dark Cloud

Haruki (third son), born in Kaunas, and Yukiko.

Nazi Army was concentrating in East Prussia. The Nazi officers were ordered to learn at least enough Russian to understand a map of the Soviet Union by the end of May.

Chiune also reported that German tanks were mobilizing on the border between Germany and the Soviet Union. A road in Lithuania was the border. Soviet tanks were moving out to protect the Lithuanian border and both armies were waiting. The Soviet Union made the deserted area between East Prussia and the Soviet Union wider. The people in that area were evacuated and the Soviets set up numerous observation towers along the three to five kilometer front line. On April 15, a large amount of grain was brought from Minsk. The atmosphere was reported to be tense. It seemed to me the facts he reported conveyed increased tensions.

Due to the growing tensions, more restrictions and curfews were being enforced. In September 1941, an order had come down that all Jews in Germany had to wear a yellow Star of David at all times. In the evening, Jews could only walk in the city for a few hours.

"I wonder if they are okay," I thought, remembering the exhausted eyes of the Polish Jews who had come to the consulate in Kaunas. I was sure my husband was thinking the same. "All I can do for them now is pray that they arrived safely at their destinations," Chiune said. We sometimes talked about the Jews. We didn't know what happened to them until years later.

My husband's job in Königsberg was to investigate the military movements in Germany and the Soviet Union. Around the time we arrived in Königsberg, the Japanese Foreign Minister, Matsuoka, visited Europe. There, he met with German Foreign Minister von Ribbentrop, who hinted that there was a possibility Germany might fight the Soviet Union. Matsuoka stopped in Moscow on his way back to Japan, and signed the Japanese-Soviet Neutrality Pact on April 13, 1941. Since the relationship between Germany and the Soviets was getting worse, the Soviet Union was pleased with the treaty. I heard when Matsuoka was leaving Moscow, Stalin himself saw him off.

On June 22, 1941, the German Army invaded all along the battlefront from Finland to Romania. It was the largest army ever assembled for a battle. In 1941, Germany was feeling the exhilaration of military victory. The German Army, which had invaded the Soviet Union in June, arrived in Moscow in December. They came to a standstill in the snows in the suburbs of Moscow. They were soon faced with a massive counterattack by the Soviets. The German Army's involvement in a desperate battle to hold their ground was not reported in Germany.

On December 7, 1941, Japan attacked Pearl Harbor. Two weeks earlier, the Japanese diplomats in Europe received a letter suggesting that their families go back to Japan, because it

The Dark Cloud

Königsberg consulate staff and family.

would be impossible to leave Europe if Japan started a war with the United States. It was our last chance to return to Japan.

My husband told me, "the Foreign Ministry said we should send our families back to Japan." I answered, "no, I won't go. I will stay with you and my sons, even if I die," I answered. If I left Europe, I would be worried about Chiune. My children and I would feel better being with Chiune than being without him.

The news about Japan's attack on Pearl Harbor was in the morning paper. The article had a map of Japan and some explanation about the country. After breakfast, the houseboy brought in the paper. He asked, "is Japan really this small? I think I'd fall into the sea if I tripped." He was surprised. Surely the map made Japan look very small, as if it were impossible to live on that tiny island. It was unbelievable for him that such a small country would go to war with the United States. Japan, which had been unknown to ordinary Europeans, now occupied the attention of Europe. It seemed to me that most Europeans had thoughts similar to those of our houseboy.

65

Visas for Life

Hitler's biggest fear was realized when the United States joined the war against the Axis after the Japanese attack on Pearl Harbor. The Nazi Army hadn't prepared for the Russian winter. As a result, they suffered a terrible defeat in Russia in 1941 and 1942. Their efforts to capture Moscow and Stalingrad failed. Hitler concentrated his efforts on continuing his attack on the Soviet Union again the following year. Once again, the German invasion ended in defeat.

The Destruction of Berlin

"We will be defeated in this war," Chiune had said from the start. When we moved to Kaunas, we knew Japan would form an alliance with Germany. Even at that time, my husband thought Germany and Japan would be defeated. The information he had collected on the war helped him to predict the defeat of the Axis powers. Two Polish spies sometimes visited our consulate in Königsberg. Much of what Chiune learned came from these spies. Information was continuously being relayed to the Japanese government. The Foreign Ministry had a difficult time believing what Chiune reported.

Four days after Japan attacked Pearl Harbor, Germany and Italy declared war against the United States. Soon thereafter, American diplomatic institutions, as well as a mission from Latin America, were expelled from Germany.

Life in Germany changed overnight. For example, in 1942, dancing in public was prohibited, and violators were severely punished. Although diplomats were exempt from such rules, we didn't interact very much with other diplomats in Germany. The British Air Force focused on night bombing major cities in Germany and Austria.

On January 20, 1942, during secret talks of high officials in the Wannsee Conference, "The Final Solution" was outlined. According to papers written by Reinhard Heydrich, Hitler's chief policy architect of the Final Solution, the "roundup and mass slaughter of Jews in concentration camps throughout Europe" would soon take place.

I was very interested in a small movement that had formed in Germany against the Nazis. The Gestapo responded to it much more aggressively than the Japanese Military Police

The Dark Cloud

Memorial service for former German President General Hindenburg.

would have reacted. I heard from my neighbors that two students at Munich University, the leaders of the movement called *The White Rose,* had been put to death. They were a brother and sister, Hans and Sophie Scholl. Later, I heard two more leaders of *The White Rose* had been captured and killed along with many others. A monument commemorating Hans and Sophie still stands at Munich University.

Stories like this spread like wildfire. Some people who appeared to obey Hitler actually did not support him. We heard an anti-Nazi group had also been formed within the German Army. Because Germany was usually victorious in its battles against the Allied forces, these small anti-Nazi groups stopped growing.

One day, we accompanied a group of German soldiers to the grave of General Paul von Hindenburg. We watched them pray for victory. Hindenburg, who distinguished himself in World War I, was the Chief of the General Staff, and in 1925 he became the second President of the Republic of Germany. Hindenburg's grandson, a high-ranking officer, gave us his autograph on a photograph of his grave.

We enjoyed that summer swimming in the Baltic Sea. Königsberg had a lovely beach, which I visited with my chil-

Visas for Life

General Paul von Hindenburg's monument.

dren. The beach was divided into two sides. On one side of the beach, people swam with swimming suits, and on the other side, people bathed without wearing anything. It was an incredible scene for us, as we were not used to this in Japan.

I liked to look at buildings, and I took pictures of the ones I liked in town. I thought of studying architecture in Königsberg. The German government ordered us to leave after a year and a half. I knew the consulate would close before I could begin my studies.

My husband was recommended for posting in the Japanese Legation in Bucharest, Romania. The war was getting more severe and the tide was now turning against Germany. By the end of 1942, the battle in Stalingrad was drawing to an end. In February 1943, the German army surrendered in Stalingrad. The defeat was a shock, not only to Hitler and the Nazis, but also to the German people. At the same time, the bombings in German cities were becoming more intense.

In the autumn of 1942, we again visited Berlin on our way to Romania. When we passed through the city, I saw the Brandenberg gate, where I had walked two years before. It had been hit in an air raid. After only a few years, this lively city had been badly damaged. There were several air raids during the nights we spent in Berlin, and we were unable to leave our hotel. Each time an air raid siren sounded, we would run for shelter in the basement of our hotel, holding our children's hands so we wouldn't be separated. After we waited for a while in the enormous basement, which was big enough to be a parking lot, we went back to our room. As soon as we returned to our rooms, the siren would start again. This happened several times.

I met a young German woman in the elevator on one of our trips to the basement. She was a beautiful woman with long flaxen hair. "Germany will never be defeated," she proclaimed. "We will fight until the end. We will recover!" She looked a little pale and muttered this many times. Her eyes looked like she was praying, and her voice was the only sound heard in the elevator. In this woman, I saw a German patriot, proud of her country. Her nationalistic fanaticism deeply troubled me.

The tide continued to turn against Germany. Mussolini was overthrown in a coup in July 1943. In France, the Resistance movement against Germany gained momentum. In May 1943, the United States and the British Allied Forces defeated the German army in North Africa.

In April of 1945, the Soviet Union occupied Königsberg and changed the city's name to Kaliningrad. I heard that the Germans living there were deported.

Our family moved to Romania with the feeling that we were witnesses to much of the suffering and devastation brought on by the war.

Chapter 4

A Foreboding of Defeat

The King Who Had Forgotten How to Laugh

IN 1943, the German Army was stationed in Bucharest. I was surprised to see German soldiers marching proudly in town, because Germany was on its way to defeat after its losses in Russia. It seemed to me that these German soldiers were showing us they had not completely lost their dignity. A German officer wearing impressive decorations on his chest and an Iron Cross led the soldiers. He walked erect and reminded me of a splendid Japanese war commander. My impression of Bucharest was that the buildings were painted the same way they were in Germany. At German-occupied headquarters in Bucharest, a German flag hung from the window, along with a large photograph of a general who was the German military commander in charge of Romania. Passers-by could easily see the picture and the flag from the street.

When my husband left Königsberg for his new post in Bucharest, his superior, Ambassador Oshima, had given him the rank of Minister. However, the former Minister was still posted in Bucharest when we arrived. The escalation of the war around Romania had prevented him from leaving for Japan. Because of this, my husband was not able to work formally as Minister, and ended up translating Russian at the Japanese Legation. For two years, we led a rather quiet life. Beside my husband and myself, the Japanese Legation in Bucharest consisted of the Minister and his wife, and the Assistant Military Commander Nomura and his White Russian wife. There were four or five other officers as well, so we never lacked companionship.

Since I was not assigned the serious duties of a minister's wife, I was able to enjoy socializing in an informal way with the other international diplomats in town. In Bucharest, there was an active association of diplomats which published a social magazine containing the photographs of each diplomat and his wife. I had a picture taken for that magazine upon our arrival in Bucharest. The photographer who came to the Legation was a friendly German woman who showed me how to operate her camera.

In Bucharest, I usually attended diplomatic social occasions dressed in a *kimono*. The well-known Romanian artist, Nego Shano, heard about this, and asked to paint me in my *kimono* for an upcoming exhibition. I consented with pleasure. On my first day as a model for Nego Shano, he stared at me sitting in my chair. Suddenly, he advanced and pulled up the collar of my *kimono*. It apparently looked strange to him that I wore my *kimono* with the collar down, because people dressed in Western clothes wore their collars up around their necks. "We wear the *kimono* like this in Japan," I said. "You do?" he responded. But every time I sat for him, he pulled up the collar of my *kimono*. I soon found it was not easy to be a model for

A Foreboding of Defeat

Chiune and Yukiko in consulate

an artist creating an oil painting. I had to sit for long periods of time without moving. Sitting quietly is not something at which I am very good. I made a good effort because of the enthusiasm Nego Shano showed when visiting the Legation everyday. The war intensified, and he was forced to stop working before the painting was completed.

I did not have formal duties on a daily basis, so I began learning how to play the Russian guitar. The Russian guitar is smaller than a classical guitar, and has seven strings and a clear high-pitched sound. I also dreamed of learning to play the harp, but I could not find a teacher in Bucharest. My children had been studying the violin, and they also played the accordion. My husband hoped our family would one day give a family concert.

Our children were growing up. When we moved to Romania, Hiroki was eight years old, and Chiaki was six. Haruki, who was born in Kaunas, was four.

Our first residence in Bucharest was an impressive mansion on one of the major streets. One day, our maid decided my three sons should meet some of our neighbors. She took them, with their accordions in hand, and introduced them to the people on the first and second floors. She let my sons play their accordions for the neighbors. The maid showed the boys off proudly. The people the boys were introduced to would say, "they are lovely." The neighbors gave my boys chocolate and other sweets. Our maid, whose name was Pika, loved the children. After she finished introducing the boys to the neighbors in the mansion, she went outside and walked around on the street with them, and said to people, "Look at these lovely children." People on the street came up to the children and talked with them. This behavior was common in Romania, but very different from life in Japan, where people do not talk to strangers.

Pika was the name of a famous actress in Romania, and our maid wanted to be an actress. That's why she had said, "call me Pika," when I first asked her name. She was a capable woman who spoke French, German, and English. She worked hard, and during the day wore clothes which she could get dirty. On the evenings when we had guests, however, she always wore a black uniform with a white lace collar. She spoke in French if the guests spoke French and served us well at these special receptions.

One day, Hiroki, who was eight at the time, brought a lovely girl to our home and introduced her to us. "This is my girlfriend," he told us. The girl lived next door. Hiroki was a very gregarious person, and the two children quickly became good friends.

Once, when my children and I went driving in Bucharest, we met the Romanian king, Mikhail. He had an unusual story; he was called "the king who had forgotten how to laugh."

A Foreboding of Defeat

In Japanese traditional kimono, New Year's Day

When his grandfather, King Ferdinand, had died, Mikhail's father, Prince Carol, was denied the throne for being in love with a commoner. So six-year-old Mikhail had ascended to the throne. Three years later, Carol came back to Romania, demanded the throne, was reinstated, and became King Carol II. King Carol's ascension to the throne was on the condition that he divorce his common wife, Magda Lupescu. After he became king, however, Carol violated the agreement and renewed his relationship with Magda Lupescu.

Because Mikhail was used as a pawn in this political game, it was said he had forgotten how to laugh. When he finally became king a second time, he was known as The King Who Had Forgotten How to Laugh.

The afternoon we met the King, he was driving alone, wearing dark glasses. As he got out of his car, my children also came out of a car and they fell down on the street in front of the King. The King, who had forgotten how to laugh, smiled when he saw my children stumbling.

On memorial day, King Mikhail paraded along the main street on which we lived. It was a beautiful street lined with roses. We were able to watch the parade from our window. Later during our stay in Bucharest, we moved to a house at the edge of town. There was a beautiful lake across the street from that house. My children went swimming in it every day during the summer.

Bucharest was a simple city and the Romanians are a very cheerful people. Each spring we had visits from "The Dog Woman" and the big bears. "The Dog Woman" was someone who liked dogs so much that she took in many abandoned strays. She was a poor woman, and it was difficult for her to feed all her dogs. She would occasionally come into the city during the spring with her dogs and let them perform on the street corner for money. Other people brought bears into Bucharest from the countryside and made them dance. This sort of street entertainment was common in Bucharest.

In Bucharest, people spent their summers at country cottages or in villas, so when summer came around our family also looked for a villa to rent. On our first summer, it was hard to find a villa, since we had arrived only recently in Bucharest. We were finally successful, and found a cottage on the outskirts of town which was a one-hour drive from Bucharest. It was a beautiful white building with a large garden. Roses bloomed along one side of the cottage and there was an avenue of poplars along the other side. In the back, between the rose garden and the poplars, was a large garden. Beyond the garden was a lake with a boat ready to use at all times.

We would go driving on Sundays. We visited rural areas and saw farmers on their way to church. Sometimes a herd of

A Foreboding of Defeat

The Sugihara family in Bucharest, Romania. Clockwise: Haruki, Chiune, Hiroki, Yukiko, Chiaki, and Setsuko. 1944.

Visas for Life

Snowman. Bucharest, Romania.

sheep would come down a hill like a white cloud. On festival days, the rural people danced in brightly colored costumes.

Romania abounded in fruits. In Bucharest, growers set up tables along the side of the street and sold grapes. They washed the grapes in water set beside the tables, and people ate them while walking down the street. Farmers also sold homemade wine. We drank wine everyday at home. My husband liked alcohol and enjoyed having a glass of whiskey with me in the evening.

In winter, snow fell consistently on Romania. We skied often because it didn't take us long to get to the slope from where we lived. We would simply dress in our ski wear and go skiing among the pine trees. In Bucharest, the children made snowmen. Unlike the round-shaped Japanese snowmen, Romanian snowmen were shaped like real people.

In Romania, everyone said that there was a big difference between the rich and the poor. When we first arrived, I was surprised at the size of a bank note in comparison to its value. "Why is it so big?" I asked one of the maids. She answered, "A larger piece of paper makes people feel as though they have more."

In July 1944, about two years after we moved to Bucharest, an attempt was made to assassinate Hitler. On August 25 the German Army surrendered in Paris. It was clear to everyone that Germany would lose the war. It was only a matter of time.

When Allied bombing increased in the German-occupied cities of Europe, we decided to build a bomb shelter in the empty space next to our house. Just as we finished building it, the United States starting bombing Bucharest. We began to experience the fighting first-hand. The first time we were going into our shelter, our neighbors saw us and asked if they could share the bomb shelter with us. They had not built their own shelter. We all got together in the shelter and waited until the air attack finished.

The air attacks got increasingly worse. Among the officers of the Japanese Legation, our family was the only one with children. The other officers lived in Bucharest without their families. The city was dangerous, and many people told us we should move. We decided to rent a cottage in Poiana Brasov in order to avoid the bombings in Bucharest. Poiana Brasov was on a hill near the town of Brasov. It was famous for its country cottages.

As we were leaving Bucharest, Pika looked troubled. When I asked her what was wrong, she said, "I'd like to take my sewing machine, but it's too heavy." We couldn't take it with us to Poiana Brasov, and Pika lived in the country, far from Bucharest, where she couldn't transport her sewing machine without a car. I asked our driver to transport Pika's sewing machine to the country for her. Pika appreciated it and kept saying, "I have never before met such a nice person who would do this sort of thing for me."

Escape Through a Smoke Screen

The bombing on Bucharest increased. It was terrible. By the time we left the city for the cottage in Poiana Brasov, most of Bucharest had been destroyed. We once went through the city after an air raid and saw a car that had been blown onto the roof of a building by the blast of a bomb. The day we evacuated Bucharest, we got information that an air raid was imminent. My husband said, "we had better leave quickly before it starts." Somehow, in great haste, I managed to get our belongings in the car, and we left town.

    Along the road from Bucharest to Brasov, we encountered huge clouds of smoke in the road. "What is this?" Hiroki asked, as he pointed to the smoke. My husband answered, "the Germans have created a smoke screen." Chiune could not hide the tension in his voice, although he tried not to sound too distraught. Before long there was smoke everywhere in the surrounding landscape. It was impossible to see more than a few feet in any direction. We were frightened! Our car raced through the smoke heedlessly. There were important oil fields between Bucharest and Brasov, which was the target of Allied bombing that day. If oil fields were destroyed, the German Army would not be able to refuel their transportation vehicles. So the Germans created clouds of smoke around the area to prevent Allied planes from seeing their targets. As a result, we could not see the road or anything else around us. If we were hit, we wouldn't be able to do anything. It would be the end. We passed through the smoke screen at full speed and somehow got through safely.

    We drove up from the town of Brasov and arrived at our cottage on the hill. We finally felt some relief. The town of Brasov had also experienced an air raid that day. Fortunately nothing had happened to our hill. We hoped we would be safe. Then the radio announced that Allied airplanes were returning to bomb the area again. I lay on the grass in the garden and watched the sky. I spotted an American bomber flying in the distance. We were safe that day, because our cottage was located in a quiet place in the forest.

    Brasov experienced another severe air raid. "Today's air raid was especially big," my sister told me. I wanted to see what had happened to Brasov with my own eyes, so I decided to go into town with my sister. I knew my husband would stop us if I told him where we were going, so I didn't tell him anything. We drove through Brasov and saw the damage. It was a horrible example of the tragedy of war. First I saw the bodies of people who had been killed in the bombing being carried

A Foreboding of Defeat

My autographed photo of Jean Sibelius, Finnish composer.

away in a truck. Then I noticed something on the road. My sister got out of the car to get a closer look. She screamed and ran back to the car. It was the leg of someone who had been killed. The scene was the same everywhere.

Fortunately, we were safe for a while on our hill in the countryside. My husband sometimes went to the Japanese Legation in Bucharest. One day, a house boy looked at me with a strange face after I saw my husband off to work. I asked him what was wrong. He inquired, "Are you fighting with your

Romania 1942. At the steps of our home in Bucharest.

husband?" European women hug and kiss their husbands good-bye and seem unwilling to part from them even for a short while. I said good-bye to my husband when he left, and didn't kiss him. The boy misunderstood our behavior as being unfriendly.

Our peaceful life in the countryside didn't last for long. One day my husband said, "We have to leave soon." It was the end of March 1944, and the Soviet Army had invaded Romania. Under Prime Minister Antonescu's administrative power, Ro-

A Foreboding of Defeat

mania had joined the German army when they invaded the Soviet Union in 1941. They annexed Transylvania, which was a part of the Ukraine in the Soviet Union. Then in 1944, the Soviet Union recaptured Transylvania and came across the border into Romania.

It seemed to me that my husband expected the Soviet Union to invade Romania. The German Army was slowly falling to the attacking Soviets. We knew that if the Soviets attacked Bucharest, we wouldn't be able to go back there again. I was worried about a phonograph record and a picture I had left in Bucharest. They were treasures given to me by the composer, Sibelius, during our first European post in Helsinki, Finland. I thought I had better go and retrieve them while I still could, so I asked the driver to take me. It was already May.

On the way to Bucharest, our car broke down. A German army car stopped and offered me a ride. I accepted and told my driver, "please pick me up after you get the car fixed." I got into the German car. As the car approached Bucharest, we met a German soldier standing in the road. We asked him what had happened. He explained, "the fighting has now reached Bucharest. The German Army has already been defeated." The German soldier driving the car didn't know that. He asked, "do you think we can go into Bucharest?" The soldier on the road replied, "it is impossible for anyone to go into the city now. It is very dangerous here. You had better go into the forest." It was impossible for me to go back to our country cottage by myself, so I reluctantly went into the forest with the soldiers. Trucks and other military cars full of retreating German soldiers were all over the forest. Suddenly, I found myself with one of the German Army units that had been defeated in Bucharest. They were retreating for the German border. We drove through the forest trying to avoid soldiers who were running around with guns. We stopped when we arrived in a place where many trucks were parked.

"Please stay here," said the soldier who was driving. He left the car without listening to my answer. I was left by myself and could only look around. Some soldiers shouted into radios. A nearby car filled with more soldiers left hastily. Apparently, they were going scouting at the order of their commanding officer. Some soldiers were sitting, others standing and talking. It seemed as though they couldn't see me. In the distance, I could hear the sounds of guns and shelling. It was as if I were watching a movie on the screen. It was hard to believe the scene all around me.

Suddenly, the door of the car opened and the soldier who had been driving said, "the road is closed and we won't be able to get out of this forest for a while." He explained the situation to me. The Romanian resistance fighters were waiting to ambush the German Army which had been defeated and chased from Bucharest. To protect themselves, most of the German army, which had occupied Romania, left the roads and rushed into the forest. With the invasion of Romania by the Soviet Union, the national group opposing Prime Minister Antonescu, who was pro-German, made its move for power. Under the leadership of King Mikhail, they successfully achieved a *coup d'état* in August 1944. When Prime Minister Antonescu lost his power, Romania made an armistice agreement with the Soviet Union in September 1944, declaring war against Germany.

I didn't want to be alone in the car, so I got out and walked among the trees. Suddenly I asked myself, "what will happen to me?" The faces of my smiling and carefree children appeared in my mind, as well as the face of my husband, which looked worried for me.

Feeling distracted, uncertain and frightened, I stood under the shining leaves. When I came out of my reverie, I saw a man standing before me. His German-style officer's hat, blue officer's uniform, and Iron Cross registered one at a time. He was a young officer who held his head high. "Can you speak German?" he asked. His voice was tense. "Yes," I answered in German. Then his look softened. "Where are you from?" I could not answer because his height intimidated me. "The partisans are surrounding the forest," he continued. "It's so dangerous that we can't get out." I nodded and was still at a loss for words. "Is it?" was all I could muster. "We are waiting for an opportunity so we can cross the border back into Germany," he said. "Anyway, it is impossible for you to get out of this forest by yourself. I think that it's safer for you to leave with us." I nodded a little. His words were strong. I would be unable to leave that forest and go back to the cottage in Brasov by myself. The young officer took me to a car which was parked away from the other cars and said, "Please get in.

A Foreboding of Defeat

You can use this car as your house." Then he left.

Before long, it started to get dark. A soldier brought me a meal consisting of tough bread and steaming, greasy soup with vegetables and meat in a deep aluminum dish. I didn't like the smell of the soup, and put my spoon down after I had eaten two spoonfuls. The darkness of night came in silence and the young officer brought me a blanket. I lay down on the rear seat with the blanket and fell asleep. I woke up just moments later. I wondered how many restless nights I would have to spend in that car. I spent the next day in the forest. The young officer named Dürer who was responsible for me visited several times during the day. We talked quite a bit.

The German border was very close. Germany was just on the other side of the Carpathian Mountains. It must have been hard for Dürer to stay hidden in the forest when he knew his own country was so close. He seemed intrigued with me. He listened attentively as I told him I came from Japan and had a husband stationed at the Legation in Bucharest. I told him about my three children.

Several days passed in this way. I kept thinking of my husband and my children. I couldn't do anything to communicate with them. The car was reserved for my use. The other soldiers didn't come near it. Except for the time I spent talking with the young officer, I sat in the silence of the forest and thought of my children.

One afternoon as I sat in the car, I heard someone say, "guten tag." I opened the door of my car and saw an old officer. "May I come in?" he asked. I allowed him to enter. No one in the forest said, "Heil Hitler!" The old officer said, "this is a good place, here. It's quiet." He looked as though he was thinking quietly. "I had two children, but they were killed in the war," he mumbled slowly as I listened. "That's too bad," I said. "How about your wife?" "She is in my country now," he said. "She is lonely." His voice was quiet and sad. His dignified military uniform could not hide the old officer's sadness. He sat quietly for a while and then started talking again. This time he talked only about himself. Then he left. I told the young officer, Dürer, about him. Dürer said with a smile that there were other officers who had wanted to talk with me. Dürer's face was no longer that of an officer. It was the face of a lively youth.

Visas for Life

There was a hut in the center of the forest and inside it was a simple shower room made of logs. I used the shower without hesitation. The water wasn't very hot. The weather during the day was still warm. In spite of the fact that terrible fighting continued nearby, time seemed to stand still as the quiet days in the forest passed.

The soldiers sat on the grass gloomily, as their pride and hope seemed to fade away. One young officer who was in the German Air Force had frightened many people in air battles. I now wondered if he would ever fly again.

One night, after a windstorm, Dürer opened the door of my car and got in. When I saw his face, I knew the time I feared had come. It was time to leave the forest. "Thank you for protecting me," I said to his rigid profile. But in my heart, I was thinking, "if we leave here, one of us will die." He said, "you are most welcome. I enjoyed your company. Thank you. I will never forget this time we had together." He offered me his hand. We held hands tightly and tears streamed down our faces.

Instructions to leave broke the silence of the night. "We, the German Army, will leave for the border now." Dürer sat in the driver's seat and asked me to sit next to him. "Don't worry," he said. "Now, let's go." It was the same strong officer's voice which I had heard when I first met him. Strangely, I felt no fear for the fighting that was about to begin. The military cars started one by one from many points in the forest and proceeded in order. The stars were shining brightly in the sky.

In the Bombardment

As soon as our car got on to the paved road, I could hear the bombing in the distance. Almost immediately, we were in the middle of it. The sounds of the shells in the night sky shook the trees. Moments later we saw flashes. The line of trucks, army jeeps, and tanks advanced through the bombardment. Red flames exploded in the dark and we were attacked. One of the shells hit a truck full of soldiers and the truck caught fire. The soldiers jumped out of the truck and desperately tried to get into the vehicle in front of them. One soldier died, then another. Those who escaped death continued moving in silence.

A Foreboding of Defeat

The bombardment stopped for a while. As I turned around to look at the flames of the truck against the dark sky, I saw a group of soldiers standing nearby. The scene, like a magical illusion lit by flames, burned an unspeakable sadness into my mind.

The night sky burned red in the distance and the violent shelling began again. "Get out of the cars," I heard a voice calling. We stopped at once and the soldiers jumped from their cars and lay down in the short grass along the road. "Let's get out of the car." I followed Dürer's voice. We lay down in the grass with the other soldiers, as a pillar of flames shot up from the ground beside me. I felt weight on my back as I lay in the grass. Dürer was protecting me by covering me with his body. Tears flowed from my eyes.

We waited until the shelling stopped and advanced a little further.

Then it began again. We jumped out of the car, and lay down in the grass again; we repeated this several times. I slipped and hurt my ankle getting out of the car. Dürer ran with me and supported me.

The shells and bullets came again. A soldier running in front of me was shot and fell down. I almost tripped over him as I rushed through the grass. The shelling worsened. The sounds of the bullets hitting the road echoed all around us. The Germans had used up almost all of their ammunition in repelling the attack. The soldiers fell one by one. We thought we would not survive this ordeal.

Then we found ourselves surrounded by Romanian partisans. I was able to see the face of one enemy partisan who was aiming at me. When I caught his eye, he looked at me with a strange face while still aiming at me. It must have been strange for him to see a Japanese woman with the German Army. When I looked back toward him, he left without shooting me.

While I lay in the grass, I thought of my children. In my mind, the sounds of the battlefield were gone and I imagined that I was back at the cottage. Hiroki, who hared his father's interest and aptitude for speaking and learning languages, was telling me what he saw that day. My second son, Chiaki, was smiling. Haruki, my third son, sat sleepily on my sister's lap. A happy family in the bright room....

Visas for Life

Dürer's officer's insignia of rank (German Air Force).

The shelling became more intense as sounds of battle passed over my head. The young officer protected me with his body, as I closed my eyes and held my breath. The noises made by bullets grazed my vacant mind. When I came to, I was alone on the grass and I no longer felt Dürer's weight on me.

The attack had completely stopped. I looked around and saw Dürer lying near me covered with grass. I touched his hand timidly and called his name. He didn't answer.

In the soft light of dawn, I could see that Dürer had been killed. He had a smile on his face, and he looked as though he were just sleeping. There was silence all around. It was as though everybody had died. The fighting ended at daybreak. Some of the other soldiers came up to me. Many of them were injured, with blood flowing from their hands and legs. They buried young Dürer's body. "See you again, someday, somewhere without war, somewhere in the universe...." I knelt and offered my prayer to the ground where Dürer lay. I stood feeling empty in the wind that moved me like the sea.

"We will cross the border by foot." I came to my senses when I heard the messenger speak. But I was not going to the border for which the soldiers were headed. They were all expressionless and started walking and dragging their feet. These were not the same proud and confident soldiers I remembered from just a few days before.

I saw the soldiers off, and then started walking down a path that left the road. I felt something was wrong with my foot. I looked down and realized that the heel of my high-heeled shoe had been broken. I hadn't noticed it before because I had been running frantically under the attack. Every time I took a step, my body shook. My throat was scorched and exhaustion completely overtook me. I continued walking, possessed by the realization that I was alive and that I had to continue walking.

Lost on the battlefield,
Only in the dawn light
To discover the heel of my shoes missing;
How, how to escape now?

Suddenly my eyes filled with tears and I sat down. The young officer who saved my life was no longer with me. Dürer was lying in a field in a foreign country, without a headstone. My heart almost broke with this terrible sadness.

When I wiped my tears away, I saw a small farmer's house in the distance. I decided to ask the way to Brasov. I reached the farmer's house with difficulty. As soon as I knocked on the door, it opened and a gun was pointed at me. An arm reached out, grabbed me, and dragged me into the house. The door slammed. When I realized they were partisans, it was too late. They were all armed. They surrounded me and poked me with their guns.

"I am the wife of a Japanese diplomat," I shouted, but they didn't react. They didn't talk and continued poking me with their gun barrels. I couldn't speak much Romanian. I decided I shouldn't speak German, so I spoke in Russian. They only looked at me suspiciously. It seemed as if they didn't hear me. They were probably saying, "Shut your mouth!" But I repeated, "I am the wife of a Japanese diplomat."

"Your hair is not black. Your face is not yellow, either." I was able to understand what they were saying. "A Japanese has slanted eyes and ties her long hair back. This woman is not Japanese. She could be a spy." Born in the north, I have brown hair and my skin is whiter than that of other Japanese. These men had probably never seen a Japanese woman before. It was impossible for them to believe that this woman, who had come from the forest where the German Army had fought, was Japanese.

Their faces were serious and their eyes were suspicious. They looked as if they would shoot me on the spot. It seemed to me that they were still excited from the battle they had just won. But I could not cry out to beg for my life. I continued to stand there as they pointed their guns at me.

After a while, the guns began to cut into me and I thought I would be shot. My legs were shaking. "Shoot me, if you want. I am Japanese," I shouted at them in Japanese. They were apparently surprised to hear this, because they lowered their guns. "Bring someone here who can speak German or Russian," I said. They sent a man out to look for someone. We were in the Romanian countryside and it was not easy to find someone who spoke German or Russian.

That evening a young man finally came who spoke German. I told him what had happened to me and he understood. "Excuse us. Please have a seat," he said pointing at a chair. I had been standing since morning, surrounded by fighting men. All my strength was now gone. I was finally able to relax a little. As the young man relayed my story to the other men, they too relaxed. After a while, they even laughed.

The men took me to the village leader. A dinner and bath were prepared for me. They kindly said, "please stay here tonight because it is so late. We will take you to your cottage tomorrow." I said, "thank you." I was able to sleep well that night. Eight days had passed since I rushed into the forest with the German Army, and I hadn't slept much during that time.

The next morning, I was taken back to my cottage by car. To get around Bucharest through Brasov, we followed the

A Foreboding of Defeat

Nazi Gestapo and SS officers with Japanese diplomat.

mountain road to Poiana Brasov. The sight of the cottage where my husband and children were waiting cheered me up. They were waiting for me at the entrance. I arrived home wearing the uniform of a German soldier. I was surprised when I saw my husband's face. He had always been a little overweight, but he had suddenly become very thin.

My husband had been looking for me from morning until evening during the eight days that I had been missing. He said he was often stopped by the Soviet Army and had guns pointed at him. If he hadn't said anything, he would have been shot immediately. Since he was able to speak Russian, he survived. When he explained to them that his wife had disappeared, they joined him to look for me. But Chiune knew nothing about my whereabouts and had no hints. He thought that I may have been killed, but he still continued to look for me.

"Where have you been?" Hiroki asked. As I often went out for social diplomatic purposes, he thought that I had been somewhere doing just that. I held my children. I was laughing, but I couldn't stop the tears. All I could think was, "Home! I finally made it home!"

91

Diplomats of a Defeated Country

"We will go back to Bucharest," Chiune said after he hung up the phone with the Japanese Legation. It was the end of July 1945. He didn't say anything else, but I understood that he was worried. On April 30, Hitler had committed suicide. There was a demand in the Potsdam Declaration that Japan surrender. We had not yet received instructions from the Foreign Ministry in Tokyo. We also had problems communicating with Ambassador Oshima in Berlin.

We packed our belongings quickly and left for Bucharest. When we entered the city, it was full of Soviet soldiers. They walked along the same road the German Army had recently marched.

I saw Soviet soldiers take watches away from Romanians. Some of the soldiers who were wearing three or four watches were obviously enjoying them.

One morning, Soviet soldiers arrived on short notice. We had been warned by the Japanese military officer that they would come for us eventually, so we had already packed our belongings. We were escorted by armed soldiers to the military officer's residence. They informally confined my family there, along with a Military Attaché and Vice Military Attaché Nomura and his wife. They confined other officers and diplomats to other parts of the Japanese Legation. We, who had lived magnificently in the Japanese Legation, were now being confined within Soviet walls.

There were some guards around the Legation, who were Romanian and they were not very strict. A few kind soldiers brought a turtle for my children and made a house for it with stones. We had our freedom inside the residence, but were not allowed to go outside. Several days passed. The children were allowed to go out to play. Quickly, my children became friends with the children next door and spent their days playing innocently. Only the smiles of my children made me happy in that restricted life. I was also able to talk over the fence with the woman next door.

By that time, everyone thought that the Soviet Union would declare war against Japan. At the beginning of July, the Japanese government asked the Soviet Union to form a commission for ending the war. The Soviet Union refused to do this.

A Foreboding of Defeat

Our country home in Poiana Brasov, Romania. 1944.

We had not heard from Ambassador Oshima in Germany for some time.

The fact that the Soviet Union seemed prepared to continue the war created a stir in our life at the military officer's residence. On August 9, 1945, the Soviet Union declared war on Japan. The Japanese military officer named Shimonuki gathered everyone in the hall and told us, "if the Soviets relocate us, I will kill you all with my sword. As Japanese, we cannot live in disgrace, so please be ready for that." As he talked, he held a long Japanese sword in his hands. From then on, even at the dinner table, he held the sword. We were afraid he would kill us.

"Should we escape? I don't want to be killed here," my husband said half joking. Half in jest, I too was thinking of escaping confinement. I was more afraid of the Japanese officer than of the Soviets. I heard after the war that many people had committed suicide in Manchuria. If the Soviet soldiers had taken us at that time, we might have been killed by the military officer's sword.

One day, Hiroki, who was playing outside, came home with a bloody nose. "Let's talk about which country will be defeated when we meet again," I heard him say to another boy. The boys used to play war. Hiroki said that while they were playing, they fought over whether or not Japan would be defeated. "Japan will never be defeated," Hiroki had asserted. Another child had thrown a stone at him. But children forgive, and the boys played together again the next day.

On August 15, the news was in the paper that Japan had accepted the Potsdam Declaration. "The Soviet soldiers will come again," my husband said. He didn't mention anything about the defeat. He had known Japan would be defeated, but as a Japanese citizen, he didn't want to accept the fact that it had happened.

It was clear that we wouldn't be allowed to stay in Romania, so I had the maid pack our belongings. I gave my *kimonos* to my friends. It seemed to me the children didn't really understand what had happened, but unexpectedly they too started packing their belongings.

The next day, the woman from next door spoke to me in a low voice. "If the Soviet soldiers take you and your husband away, give your children to me over the fence immediately." Things were happening very quickly, and I could barely understand what she was talking about. I didn't say anything. "The situation for Japan is bad now," she added. If the Soviets send you and your family to Siberia, it will be very bad for your children. I will take the responsibility for bringing them up." This woman had three children of her own, and they were good friends with my sons. My sons were popular in the neighborhood, and she said that she had decided to divide my children among three neighboring families. I thanked her for her kindness with tears in my eyes, but I couldn't bear the thought of having to leave my children.

Three days after the Japanese defeat, a Soviet officer came to us in the morning. He called my husband to the guest room. Everybody, including the military officer, stood frozen, waiting for the meeting to end. I drew my children to my breast.

After a while, my husband came out of the guest room, but he didn't look bad. He said, "we will pack our bags and go to an internment camp on the outskirts of Bucharest." We felt relieved when we heard my husband say this, and we quickly packed our belongings. The Soviet soldiers who had guarded us helped with the packing. They said, "take everything. Because the Japanese have lost, you don't have anything in Japan." I didn't know if I should appreciate their help or feel embarrassed. I told the kind woman next door what we were doing and said good-bye. We then got on a truck, and she and her family saw us off.

Chapter 5

The Internment

Days of Anxiety

OUR INTERNMENT BEGAN in a Romanian army barracks on the outskirts of Bucharest. When we arrived, the Japanese Foreign Minister of the Romanian Legation, an Italian diplomat, and some imprisoned German soldiers were already there.

Our family was housed in two rooms in a large building. Our two oldest sons and Setsuko stayed in one room while I, my husband, and our youngest son, Haruki, stayed in the other. A coal stove warmed the room, but the dirt floor and straw mattress made the room rather uncomfortable. We had grown accustomed to the luxury of thick carpets and feather quilts. We suffered from sleep deprivation and the days were long and monotonous since we had nothing to do. The one activity we looked forward to was taking a walk in the barracks square.

The German prisoners were given work outside, but diplomats were not forced to work. Adjusting to such a life was difficult for Chiune, who had always been active and involved in many things. The best we could do was to remind ourselves we should be thankful for our safety, and try to adjust as well as we could to the uncertainty we had about the outcome of our internment.

Days passed monotonously into weeks; weeks into months. People became restless and irritated, not only because of the lack of proper food and comfort, but also because of the uncertainties of our future. We were anxious because we had no idea how long our current situation would last. The gloomy days became even gloomier as winter approached and the barracks were covered in snow. The Romanian soldiers attended to our needs, but we wondered why we never saw any Soviet soldiers. We pressed the Romanians for answers about how long we would be imprisoned and where we might be relocated.

The German prisoners cooked and delivered our meals, usually a kind of meat soup without any vegetables. I could barely stand to eat the food. We supplemented these inadequate meals with fruit and vegetables purchased from an old farmer who was allowed to come near our barracks. To buy food, we relied on our currency from the war, which was still legal tender. Our savings, which were in a Swiss bank, had been blocked.

Fortunately, the children were allowed to play freely among the barracks, so my children soon became friends with the children of the Romanian families in other barracks. The only comforts afforded to me during this time were my children's laughter, and, on some rare occasions, a musical concert given by the German prisoners. In striking contrast to their wartime activities, these German soldiers played the violin and piano, and sang. During these lively performances, we were able to talk freely.

In the midst of this depressing environment, our former neighbor from Bucharest came to visit. She felt sorry for my children having to face a Christmas with no gifts, and wanted to bring cheer to their Christmas. So she trudged through thick snow carrying a home-baked cake. When she got to our door, her frozen eyelashes showed her determination and commitment.

The birth of 1946 saw little change in our environment. We still had not received information from the Soviet Union about our situation. The Japanese prisoners in the camp became quieter as gloom overtook our barracks.

One March morning I saw one of our fellow inmates, a decorated and aristocratic German officer, walking around the barracks square. With his long beard glistening in the sun, he made me think that God had come to us. I wondered about this German's presence, as Germans were forbidden from exercising in the square with the others. The German who brought our meals explained that this man was a count from a distinguished German Royal family named Hohenzollern. He was closely related to the former German Kaiser, and had been told to return to Germany after the war. The officer had responded: "I am in the army. I will go with my soldiers, with whom I fought." This guaranteed his internment. The story moved me, and everyday I watched the count take his walks. I looked forward to this daily routine.

The departure of summer ushered in our second autumn in internment. Our routine of rising in the morning and quietly waiting for nightfall wore down our spirits. Then, on a snowy morning in December, a Soviet officer came to us with a message. He announced, "we will allow you to return to Japan. You will all leave immediately."

This information was representative of our experiences with the Soviets. We were often given little time to respond to new, life-altering instructions. As usual, we packed quickly and dressed the children appropriately. Because we were headed into the Soviet Union, we bundled our children in their fur coats.

"Where are we going?" Hiroki asked. He seemed sad to leave his friends. "We are going back to Japan," I explained, which brought a smile to his face. Although he was born in Japan, we had left the country before Hiroki's first birthday. Even though he didn't remember Japan, I could see from Hiroki's reaction that he felt a special connection to his native land.

We got in a truck again and drove through the deep snow past the gate of the camp. "Good-bye!" everyone cried out. My children's friends who heard we were leaving came to see us off. The children waved at us until we were out of sight. As we looked back, we saw only a veil of white snow.

Waving good-bye from the truck,
A final farewell to all their friends,
My sons call out,
"Auf Wiedersehen."

The Endless Journey

An old freight train with a passenger car attached was waiting for us when we arrived at the train station in Bucharest. We sat down on the hard wooden seats as Soviet soldiers boarded our car. Our trip had begun.

Only one stove heated the drafty car. The temperature was -45°F. We were covered in fleas and lice. As I neared the stove, my hands and chest felt warmer, but I still had shivers up and down my back. I was dressed in many layers, but I never felt truly warm. Our freight train inched its way through miles of open land. The days took us past masses of snow covered fields. There was not a single town in sight.

The other passengers in our car included the Japanese minister of the legation in Bucharest, along with his staff, and 17 people from the military office. The wives of the minister and vice officer, my sister, and I were the only women. Tanya, the wife of the vice officer, held her baby in her arms. The Japanese people from other European countries had been sent back to Japan before us. In our month-long journey, none of us talked about our situation. As we sat captive in our fur coats, fur caps, and long boots, we wondered, "where will they take us? Will we truly be allowed to return to Japan?" No facilities for bathing were provided, and we became filthy. The children were covered with fleas and lice.

We found out later that the route we had taken through Russia was ironically the same route taken by the Jews from Kaunas who had received visas from Chiune. This experience made our common connections even stronger.

Periodically the train stopped and we would hear a loud thumping noise. This was the sound of soldiers removing frozen urine from the train with a wooden stick. Anything liquid crystallized instantly as the mercury thermometer held steady at -45°F. Outside, in this severe cold, even our eyelashes froze, a sensation more painful than the cold itself. If we touched the iron fence of the train without a glove, it would sting.

"Get off the train! You are going to an internment camp." We received these instructions just as we arrived in a station. Afraid to even ask about our immediate future, we quietly loaded our baggage onto another truck. My family's belongings were difficult to carry.

As we climbed down from the truck in Odessa, we saw the Black Sea. The snow pelted the rough sea, and I felt a deep sorrow when I stood along the desolate seashore. This place, the first internment camp on our train trip, would be our new home.

Although I felt gloomy and depressed, my children's lively energy comforted me. Hiroki, who had turned nine, acted as the first son. This small diplomat, who quickly learned each new language by ear, carried our baggage ahead of us and held his brothers' hands. Our second son, Chiaki, was a small, cute, quiet boy of seven, with round cheeks. Our youngest son, Haruki, displayed a bright laugh that matched exactly the meaning of his name, which meant Bright Spirit. This little boy with long dark eyelashes charmed everyone. My children, covered in fur like baby bears, walked on their small feet throughout this long and terrible trip, not knowing the irrationality of war.

The internment camp in Odessa consisted of a single barrack. I heard two Soviet soldiers talking about a German prisoner who had recently tried to escape. "What happened to him?" one asked. The other responded, "he was captured and shot when he tried to board a ship." I felt a shiver run down my spine. My ability to comprehend a little Russian allowed me to understand this conversation. These kinds of stories made me fear a similar fate.

One day, my husband was taken to another room. I probably looked quite pale at that moment, and everyone in the room looked at me anxiously. I didn't know how long he was gone; a few minutes or a few hours. I couldn't think of anything and bit my lips until he came back to our room. "Don't worry," he said and sat down next to me. I couldn't believe that my husband had come back safely until I felt his body heat. Chiune did not tell me what had happened in that room.

In the evening, we lay down with blankets, without taking off our fur coats. I fell asleep holding my three children. A moment later, I woke up startled. "Where is my husband?" I looked around and felt relieved to see Chiune sleeping next to me. I repeated this behavior throughout the entire night. I kept thinking that my husband would be sent away during the night. Because Chiune spoke Russian, everybody thought that he might be taken somewhere deep within the Soviet Union.

Another day and still alive!
And the Sea of Odessa roars,
Yet I somehow feel safe.

Individually, the Soviet soldiers were nice to us. Since there was not a single washroom in the camp, we had to walk in the snow to a primitive washroom next to the sea. Of course, a soldier had to come with us as a guard. The soldiers probably thought that this long trip was hard on women. Once they knew I could speak Russian, some of them spoke to me on the way to the washroom. "Everybody here is the same to us, except for the Germans. We hope that you will be able to go back to Japan safely." What they said comforted me. I still remember the relief I felt when I thought about how these soldiers, who had to follow the most severe rules of their country, were individually simple and warm people.

After several weeks in this internment camp, we received instructions to leave. We loaded our trunks onto yet another train. We disembarked for another distant and snowy internment camp, as foreign to me as the first. I kept asking myself, "are we really returning to Japan?"

The soldiers inspected all of our belongings when we reached this second camp. They even poked my bar of soap several times with the sharp tips of their guns, to see if I had hidden anything inside it. They confiscated all of our books and took all three of our new cameras. I removed my photographs from their albums and hid them, but the soldiers discovered this and began to confiscate them. "Give me back the pictures of my children. They are important memories," I said, and grabbed some back. All of the snapshots of formal diplomatic ceremonies we'd gone to, as well as those of the Kaunas Jews, were taken from me. Only two pictures of the Jews standing in front of the Japanese Consulate in Kaunas remained with my children's photographs. I hid my 8mm films at the bottom of a bag, and was able to bring them back to Japan.

Our baggage contained all of our belongings. I had left many of my personal belongings in Romania, including the cut glass which I had collected in Czechoslovakia, and my favorite Persian carpet with the roses. As we moved from place to place as diplomats, we sent the large items that were too large to carry back to Japan via ship. Each time we passed through an inspection, we lost several of our precious belongings.

For more than three months, we repeated the pattern of traveling from one internment camp to another by train. Because our train car was connected to a cargo train, we repeatedly had to wait for the next cargo train to pass and pull us along. One morning, as I looked out the window of the train, I spotted some men in the distance. They were thin men with black hair, and they were carrying large logs on their shoulders. "Are they Japanese?" I asked Chiune excitedly. The people around the stove looked up.

"It's Nakhodka," he answered quietly. Nakhodka was a port near Japan. Everybody on the train had had a kind of empty look in their eyes, but they quickly came alive. We were almost home. Despite the fact that we were now completely surrounded by snow, we were relieved to have arrived in Nakhodka without anybody getting sick. Only one of our staff members had gotten frostbite.

Upon our arrival in Nakhodka on the Sea of Japan, we were inspected and placed in a large room in another internment camp. Knowing we were so close to Japan, my footsteps felt light with anticipation, and our baggage, which had been so cumbersome, suddenly seemed very manageable.

Hope

At the Nakhodka camp, the 17 of us in our group were housed in one large room. Once again, we were forbidden from going outside, so we stayed in our room all day long. We were separated from the other Japanese prisoners by a barbed wire fence. The people on the other side of the fence were forced to work cutting trees and carrying lumber. We were not to work, so we simply sat in jail, uncertain of our fate.

Although we had a stove, it was pathetically inadequate. We still lived in our fur coats. March was still very cold. Our meals consisted of only bread and soup. Without a means for exercise, the greasy soup became inedible, my appetite diminished, and we always had leftovers. "Why don't we take the leftovers to the Japanese soldiers who are prisoners next to us?" my sister suggested, and we brought some food to the fence. The Japanese soldiers approached us. "Would you like some?" we asked, passing the food over the fence. They accepted gratefully, thanking us profusely. Taking our leftovers to these men became a daily routine. It seemed as though they were always hungry. If the Soviet soldiers had known about our activities, we would have been punished, so the Japanese soldiers ate our leftovers hastily. Tobacco and rolling papers were rationed to us, so we would spend time during the day rolling tobacco into cigarettes. In the evenings, we would sneak these cigarettes to the soldiers through the fence.

"A repatriation ship came yesterday, but we couldn't get on," the Japanese soldiers told us. They had been waiting to return to Japan since they had been captured at the end of the war. Repatriation ships rarely appeared, so the number of people who could return to Japan on each ship was small. The soldiers explained that they had to follow the Soviets' instructions if they wanted to go back to Japan. "There were some who were in disfavor with the Soviets, and they were sent to the back country." I realized that Nakhodka did not mean we were safely home. We wondered when it would be our turn to leave.

One day, one of the Japanese prisoners asked me if he could borrow our violin. Since my children had taken violin lessons in Romania, we had a small one. He used it for an evening concert, which brought singing and some merriment to our bleak lives.

In Nakhodka, unlike in the other camps, we were provided plenty of hot water for showers. At the other camps, there had been a system for showering. The soldiers would shout, "soap up." After quickly using the soap, we would get hot water for a moment, and then it would be turned off. If we didn't take fast showers, we would not be able to wash. Hot water was the best thing about Nakhodka. One day, when the other women and I were showering together, the hot water stopped. When I called out, "the hot water has stopped," a group of Japanese prisoners came into the room to check the showers. We crouched down to hide our bodies. The same thing happened again the next day. "It worked well at first, so it shouldn't stop," we explained. They responded, "the shower must be broken," and continued to walk around the shower

The Internment

room. Women were probably a rare sight in the internment camp.

I remembered the German soldiers I had met in the forest in Romania, and compared these Japanese soldiers to them. As the only woman with the German soldiers, they treated me with respect. None of the German soldiers had tried to peek in at me while I showered.

A month passed quickly, but we still didn't receive any information from the Soviets about or concerning our fate. It was very difficult for us to know we were so close to Japan.

One day in April, my husband was called away. When he returned, he told me quietly, "they want your *kimono*." He said that the officer in charge of the camp wanted it for his wife. They knew from the baggage inspection that I owned a *kimono*. Since I had given most of my *kimonos* to friends in Romania, I only had this one *kimono* and *obi*. If I refused this request from the head of the camp, I feared that the hope of returning to Japan might disappear; so I decided to give up my *kimono*.

After a few days, the officer in charge said to us, "I will let you go back to Japan." Something hot ran through my body. I still remember my joy at this announcement. We packed immediately and left the camp. A small cargo ship bound for Vladivostok was waiting for us at the port. The excitement I felt climbing up the ladder onto the ship was much greater than any I could have experienced if I were taking a cruise on a deluxe ocean liner. We were loaded into the bottom of the ship, with a straight ladder that went up to the deck. I went up and down the ladder with my sister, the wife of the minister, and Tanya to get meals. The meals were still bread and soup, but we didn't mind any more. We were also allowed to shower more frequently.

Two days later, we arrived in Vladivostok. We felt relieved. As we were leaving the deck, the young officer in charge of the ship came up to us. He had come down to the bottom of the ship once in a while and talked to us through our interpreter, Chiune. He offered us his hand and said good-bye in Russian.

"Good-bye, Mr. Sugihara. Please take care. You too, Mrs. Sugihara," he now said in perfect Japanese. My husband and I were stunned by his Japanese. We had talked with him in Russian through my husband. We, the Japanese diplomats, had been very careless when speaking in Japanese. We said many things, some of them quite bad, about the Soviets. And here, he had understood everything. When I thought about that, once again I felt fearful of the Soviet Union.

We got on the Japanese repatriation ship "Koanmaru" at the port in Vladivostok. The ship was full of Japanese evacuees. People all around me were speaking Japanese, which I hadn't heard spoken by so many people in a long time. This stirred deep feelings within me about my country. At the same time, I felt as if I were listening to a foreign language.

We must have been quite conspicuous in our fur coats. Many years after the war, my first son met a man on business who told Hiroki that he had been on that ship with us and remembered us. There were so many people on the ship that we could not find a place to stand. When I saw Hakata port, I could not stop crying.

"It's Japan. We have come back to Japan." I said this several times, drawing my three children close to me. Their homeland held no familiarity to them.

While we had been traveling through Siberia, I had been afraid. Fortunately, the Soviet soldiers had appreciated my husband's Russian and had been friendly toward us. Now we had returned alive and together to our homeland.

Coming back alive from the war,
I hear my mother tongue
In a low tone all about the homeland harbor;
It sounds so sad in my heart.

Chapter Six

Bitter Suffering in Our Homeland

Advised to Resign

IN APRIL 1947, we finally stepped back on Japanese soil. It had been ten long unforgettable years since we had seen our beloved native country. We arrived at Hakata Port, and decided to first go to Numazu, where my mother lived. Numazu was closer to the office of the Foreign Ministry than Gifu, where Chiune's parents lived. We were tired and almost penniless. We could not withdraw money from our savings account in the Swiss bank. What little money we had consisted of the 5,000 yen that was paid to us as repatriates.

As we boarded the train for Numazu, we were surprised to see how crowded it was with female shoppers. As the train made stops, and more people filled the cars, it became impossible to enter or exit through the doors. In desperation, people began entering and exiting through the train windows. Some passengers were even sleeping in the baggage nets. It was quite a bizarre scene.

When we arrived at Numazu, we found out that my mother was no longer there. She had fled Numazu during the devastating air raids, and now lived in Kanuki with her sister. It was fortunate that she moved, because many of the people who stayed were killed by the air raids. The ashes of the deceased were gathered together at a temple in Numazu.

When we finally did meet with my mother, I noticed that she had aged considerably. Ours was a joyous reunion, because we had not been expected. Since my mother and aunt had not heard about us after the war, they were understandably very worried and anxious to hear what had happened to us.

We decided that it would be best to remain in Numazu. There, we could better assess the present situation and carefully determine what our next step would be. We enrolled our children in the local elementary school. At first, the boys were regarded as foreigners because they often spoke to each other in German or Romanian. It was not long, however, before they were completely accepted and made new friends. They played with their friends as though they didn't have a care in the world.

After some advice given by a friend, Chiune decided to sell the house he owned in Gifu Prefecture. From the money we received for this property, we bought a piece of land in Kugenuma, within Fujisawa City in the Kanagawa Prefecture. This property was 2,500 square feet, but we could only build a 56-square-meter house on it because of building restrictions which were imposed on everyone. Lack of raw materials was probably one of the factors limiting the size of houses then. In April 1947 a new House of Parliament had been elected. The newly elected parliament approved a new Constitution which took effect in May. Massive changes ensued in Japan. Women were given the right to vote. In addition, there was a large land reform in Japan.

Since Chiune was told that he did not have to report to the foreign office immediately, he rested for about three months. He eventually received a letter with instructions to report to the Foreign Ministry. I'll never forget the day that he returned from that appointment. He looked very tired and forlorn. With feelings of foreboding stirring within me, I asked, "what happened to you?" He answered, "I was called into the office of Vice Foreign Minister Okazaki and told, 'as we no longer have a post for you, please resign. We can no longer take you under our wing!'" We just looked at each other in silence. No words could possibly describe the pain and disappointment we experienced.

Chiune had expected this or something worse to happen eventually. However, as time went on without incident, he allowed himself some hope that he was wrong. All hope was crushed that terrible day. He quietly accepted the decision and

Bitter Suffering In Our Homeland

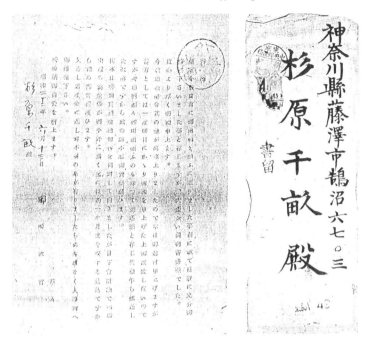

A letter to Chiune from the Foreign Ministry after his resignation.

never spoke of it again. I later learned that Vice Foreign Minster Okazaki had really said, "it is because of that incident in Lithuania. We can no longer take you under our wing." I felt that my husband was treated very badly. I wanted to express my feelings and to tell them about how dutifully and faithfully Chiune had served the Foreign Office. The Foreign Office did pay Chiune a small retirement allowance of a few hundred dollars. This was equivalent to the pre-war allowance. Because of high costs of living, the retirement money was soon gone. About that time, our savings from the Swiss bank were finally released. As a result, we were able to survive a little longer even though we were at the brink of poverty.

To make matters worse, during this low point in our lives vicious and groundless rumors were circulating among my husband's colleagues at the Foreign Ministry. The rumor was, "Sugihara should have enough money because he took payment from the Jews when he issued those visas." Throughout this dark period, Chiune remained stoic and outwardly calm.

Visas for Life

He eventually cut off all relations with these colleagues.

In the days after the war, Chiune was very depressed. It was as if a shadow had crossed Chiune's face. I often found it difficult to look at him because of this.

During the dark days of poverty, Chiune would go to Gifu whenever possible so that he could bring back some rice from the country. Rice was a luxury, because we existed on cooked sweet potatoes or regular potatoes for all our meals. We had rice only on rare occasions. Unfortunately, even with the rice, this diet was far from adequate for three growing boys.

It was very painful for me to hear the boys ask, "do you have something to eat?" We were not the only ones experiencing hunger. People throughout Japan suffered from famine. Even with strict rationing, there was an acute shortage of food. We did not, however, suffer from malnutrition because we were able to get food on the black market.

Since jobs were scarce and there was little need for anyone with skills in languages, Chiune had a difficult time finding employment. This was a time of mental anguish and disappointment for him. After serving a lifetime in the diplomatic corps, it was difficult to find oneself unemployed. It was especially hard because he was 47 years old. In desperation, Chiune contemplated peddling rice. I discouraged him from that idea because I felt that he was not suited to such a job. For a very short time, he sold light bulbs door-to-door. Throughout this worry-filled period, I did not hear one word of self-pity or complaint from him.

I had problems adjusting to this change in our lives. As the wife of a diplomat, I hadn't had much experience cleaning house or cooking in the kitchen. Along with my lack of housekeeping experience, there was a shortage of everything, such as gas, hot water, and heat. In order to cook, it was necessary to make a charcoal fire. A wood fire was needed for heating the water for bathing. Making a charcoal or wood fire was not an easy task, and I often had to get help from my neighbors. On many occasions I was reduced to tears by my frustration. The only joyous aspect of my life at that time were the happy faces of my lively children.

Unfortunately, this low time in our lives had yet to reach its lowest point. We were about to face another tragic event. One day, our youngest son, Haruki came home looking pale and tired. He had left for school that morning looking cheerful and lively. But now he complained of having a headache. I put him straight to bed and he soon fell asleep. As I sat by his bedside to keep watch on him, his nose began to bleed. We immediately called the family doctor. The doctor was very frustrated because he could not determine what was causing the bleeding or how to stop it. By now, the whole family was at Haruki's bedside, looking at his blood-stained face. We all prayed for some kind of miracle. Hiroki read the Bible, which he had never read before. The Bible belonged to Chiune, who had been baptized in the Greek Orthodox Church. Meanwhile, I prayed to god to please save my son. But my Haruki, who added brightness wherever he went, was not meant to live long on this earth. By daybreak the next day, he had left us.

Chiune went out to the garden and stood alone, looking helpless and vacant-eyed. I knew that this day would be forever imprinted in my mind. In my sorrow, I recalled that just a few days before, Haruki had come home from school and had commented brightly, "Heaven is a beautiful place. I don't want to become an adult. I'll die while I am still a child and go to Heaven. Then I will become an angel." I thought his

Haruki's funeral, November, 1947.

comment was very unusual, because we never referred to Heaven or angels, and I had never read the Bible to him. Feeling very uneasy about this strange conversation, I replied, "if you go to Heaven, I will be very sad. Don't you think so?" He thought about that for a while and then answered, "Well, I will come back again if you call me." As I went over our conversation in my mind, it occurred to me that Haruki, who was born in Kaunas, must truly have been a messenger of God. In Japanese folklore, suffering and loss of life are sometimes the by-product of doing a good deed. Perhaps he was sent to help the Jewish refugees, and now that this bright and loving messenger had fulfilled his mission, he was called back to Heaven.

Because of our poverty, we had a very simple funeral service for Haruki. Had it not been for Chiune's support, and the realization that I had two other children who needed me, I would not have had the courage to go on. This was indeed the most trying time of my life. Although our family had gone through countless hardships in the previous ten years, with the death of our beautiful child we felt that we had reached the lowest depths of our suffering.

A Second Life

It was hard to adjust to a life of poverty and hunger after a life of relative luxury. The final blow came with the loss of a precious and beloved child who was the light of all our lives. I realize now that Chiune's suffering at this time was far more acute than what I went through. Not only did he suffer the loss of a child, he suffered the indignity of losing a career that was usually assumed to be life-long. He suffered the stigma that came with groundless rumors about his taking money for visas. He faced the specter of beginning a new life while approaching the age of 50. These were at times seemingly insurmountable obstacles in his life. In his despair, he became more isolated and would not speak of these things because his hurt was so deep. However, gradually the small spark still left in him began to grow. His perseverance rose, along with his deeply ingrained fighting spirit. The code of Bushido made his spark grow. He slowly came out of his despair.

Chiune with his staff at the U.S. Military post exchange in Tokyo, 1950.

A year after Haruki's death, my dearest sister Setsuko passed away from a kidney ailment. Post-war medical care was not the best. If she had not been living in these difficult conditions, I believe she would be alive today. Not only was this a tragic loss for me, it was also a tragedy for my boys. In many ways she was as much a mother to them as I was. To this day she is missed by all of us.

Just when things were at their worst Chiune got a job. Although I personally felt it to be disgraceful to work for one's conquerors, Chiune eventually got a job as manager of the PX of the occupation forces. He got this job because of his ability to speak English. He looked at it in a practical way and soon put all of his energy and time into his new position. By doing this, he was in a sense letting go of the past and beginning anew. Since his new job dealt with food for the occupation forces, our children now were able to have a little more variety in their diet rather than to subsist on a potato diet. We were even able to get a luxury item, a telephone, which was very rare at that time.

The children were also faced with making adjustments in this new life. They had no problem with speaking and understanding Japanese because we spoke primarily in our native language at home. But they were considerably behind in reading and writing so they had to take extra lessons at their school for one year in order to catch up. For various reasons, they were not immediately accepted by their peers. For example, while most of the children wore cloth shoes and carried cloth school bags, our boys wore their leather shoes and carried leather bags. They also sometimes spoke to each other in German and Romanian. These differences set them apart but gradually they made adjustments and were soon accepted completely.

As we were all making gradual adjustments, I became pregnant and had a fourth son. I believed that our newest son may have been a reincarnation of Haruki so I named him Nobuki, which means long life.

Shortly after Nobuki was born, the PX closed and Chiune had to seek employment once again. Before long, he was offered a job by an American company named Aponje. Aponje hired him because they needed someone fluent in Russian, Japanese, and English. The company was a trading company that dealt with expensive textiles. The president of the company could speak Russian and English. He needed someone to interpret for him. Some time after working for Aponje, Chiune made an observation while we were having dinner. He said, "I thought the president was Russian, but I have heard that he is Jewish." That comment brought back to us those memories of events which took place in Kaunas. We both expressed interest in what might have been the fate of all those Jewish refugees with desperate and dirty faces. This conversation was a very rare one since Chiune never spoke of, or discussed the incident in Kaunas with me or with anyone else. He still felt the pain of losing his position in the Foreign Ministry and the hardships that followed as a result of his dismissal. He did not think that writing all those visas was anything special, so he had very little to say about the whole incident.

Chiune was a very good father to his children. He was always very understanding and kindly. He never criticized or scolded them. He preferred to speak to them in a logical and conversational manner.

Chiune encouraged Hiroki to become a governmental official. He said to him, "if you don't graduate from Tokyo Univer-

sity, you won't be accepted as a government official." I think he really wanted Hiroki to be a diplomat because he often said, "work for the Foreign Ministry." Hiroki often observed his father preparing breakfast for them in the morning. This was quite unusual in a Japanese household because it was usually done by the mother or a woman in the family. Chiune did not mind this because he was a habitually early riser. Since I suffered from low blood pressure, I was a late riser. But the fact of seeing his father prepare breakfast somehow inspired Hiroki to study harder. I think that it was one way for Hiroki to express appreciation to his father for what he was doing for them each morning.

Another incident that comes to mind and illustrates his concern for their education was the stereo set incident. One day, I overheard Chiune saying to Hiroki, "if you pass the high-school examination, I will buy you a stereo." Hiroki was then in his third year of junior high and was preparing for the entrance examination at Shonan High School. The day that we received the news that Hiroki had passed, Chiune rushed out of the house and soon returned with a big box. Of course it contained the promised stereo. At the time it was a very expensive item, but he was proud and happy to honor his promise to his son.

Contrary to my husband's wishes, I did not want my sons to work for the Foreign Ministry because I still felt resentment about the bad treatment they had given Chiune. So when Hiroki spoke of his desire to study in the United States, I did not discourage him. Hiroki went on to study at Sacramento City College and Chiaki soon followed him there. Chiune accepted their decision very philosophically and said that it was their choice to make.

I was still suffering from severe anxiety as a result of Haruki's death. This condition affected my behavior with Nobuki. I was nervous and anxious. I constantly worried about Nobuki's safety and well-being. I wouldn't even let him go outside of the garden gate to play with his friends. Predictably, my behavior affected Nobuki and he became very dependent on me. As a result, during first grade, I went to school with him until he was dismissed each day. Fortunately for him, he eventually made friends and gradually became a more independent child.

I had always loved and enjoyed writing tankas, a form of Japanese poetry. I began to study them again since I had more time to myself as my children grew older. Chiune did not encourage me to spend time with this hobby while the children were young, but now he enthusiastically encouraged me to pursue this hobby. He said, "it is good for you to have a hobby." I also always had an interest in architecture but had never had the time to study it. So when we decided to build a new house, since we had outgrown our 56-square-meter house, I decided that I would design a European-style house. While in Europe, I had always admired the beautiful architecture. When I told the carpenters that I wanted a round window with iron bars, they said, "we have never made a window like that." After I explained to them how it was made, they were able to figure out how to make one. This unusual looking window aroused the curiosity of carpenters nearby and many of them came to inspect the window. Before we began building this new house, Chiune did bring up the notion of moving to another country because he was still feeling somewhat discontented about living in Japan because of the bad treatment he had experienced. After much discussion about this issue, we finally agreed to remain in Japan for the sake of our children.

Although our situation was gradually improving, we still endured hardships. We were now living only a few minutes' walk from Kagenuma Beach. The family enjoyed sitting on the wide sandy beach as we talked about many things past, present, and future. We even fantasized about creating a Utopian kingdom on one of the many uninhabited islands nearby. Chiune visualized a kingdom ruled by rational and humane leaders. In a sense, it was a heaven on earth in which he would be the ruler and I, of course, the Queen.

During our summer vacations, relatives and their children visited with us. We have wonderful memories of those long summer days at the beach because we practically had the beach to ourselves since large crowds of people still did not go to the beach as they do today.

After working for two years at Aponje, Chiune quit his job and began working for the International Department for the Soviet Union of NHK, a national television network. He also taught Russian at Nicholi Institute. Then in 1956, he started working for the Science and Technology Agency. There he translated literature from Russian, English, German, and French. He also recorded and translated a commercial movie for the Soviet Union at the information center of the Science and Technology Agency. Finally in 1960, he was asked to work for the Kawakami Trading firm as head of the Moscow office because of his fluency in Russian. I expected to move to Moscow also because I had always gone with him whenever he moved. I asked, "shall I go with you?" Chiune had previously given this move a great deal of thought. For the first time he said, "no, you should not because it's not easy to enter the Soviet Union or to travel freely. It will also be very boring for you and it's very cold there." His concerns for my health and well-being were the deciding factors which prompted him to go to Moscow by himself.

In a Faraway Country

Kawakami Trading Company had started trading with the Soviet Union after World War II. Chiune's job with the company in Moscow was to buy crude oil from the Soviet Union for Japanese fishing boats. This was done in cooperation with the

Chiune in Moscow, 1965.

All Fisherman's Association, a co-op of Japanese fisherman and their boats. Kawakami Trading Company was purchasing C-grade oil for this use. Zenkoh Suzuki was chief of the All Fisherman's Association at this time. He later became prime minister of Japan.

While living in Moscow, Chiune stayed at the Hotel Ukraine

and commuted to his office by car. Being a methodical and careful driver, the traffic control office had to shout to him, "drive faster!" almost everyday until he became more accustomed to the quick pace of driving in Moscow.

Chiune was also aware that he was under close scrutiny by the KGB, as were most foreigners. Whenever he left his hotel room, he always left his keys at the front desk because he suspected the hotel acted as informants to the KGB. His telephone and telegrams were also monitored. As a businessman, however, Chiune did not feel the same anxiety and pressure he'd previously experienced, being under constant surveillance, as a Consul in Europe.

By now, Chiune had lived more of his life in foreign countries than he had lived in Japan. Japan was changing rapidly and the tempo of life was getting faster and faster. In contrast, life in Moscow remained relatively slow. Chiune probably enjoyed living in Moscow over living in Japan. He was very comfortable with the Russian language. He was also accustomed to Russian customs, so his adjustment to life in Moscow was a relatively easy one. Eventually, he held the longest record for being stationed in Moscow as a businessman from Japan. An example of how much he blended into Soviet culture was his love of Russian music. He had not been particularly fond of popular Japanese music, but he became an avid fan of the Darkdaks, a popular Japanese four-man group that sang popular Russian folk songs. He often sang songs by the Darkdaks, and attended their concerts whenever possible.

Since many of the Japanese business representatives in Moscow had learned Russian from Chiune in Harbin Gakuin, they addressed him as Sensei (teacher). On one occasion when Hiroki, our eldest son, went to visit his father in Moscow, he met many of Chiune's colleagues at a restaurant. He observed that many of them addressed his father as *Sensei*. They were all very comfortable and at ease with Chiune as they chatted happily about a trip they had all enjoyed to Shanghai. Chiune was also able to find employment for many of his former students at Harbin Gakuin. After the war, an annual meeting was held of Harbin alumni, so Chiune always received notices about upcoming events. Even the Japanese ambassador in Moscow at this time had been Chiune's junior while he was in the Manchurian Ministry. Having contact with former alumni, students, and colleagues from Harbin, Chiune was very secure, comfortable, and happy living in Moscow.

Temperatures of -30° F were normal for winters in Moscow. In fact it was considered relatively warm, when compared to other regions of Russia. When the temperature dropped below -30° F, all of the schools were closed. Chiune was able to adapt easily to cold weather because he had lived so many years in the cold northern countries of Europe. He also enjoyed taking winter walks in the white birch forests in the suburbs of Moscow. When the birch were covered with snow, the blanket of white transformed the forest into a beautiful, soundless, and mysterious place that Chiune loved. He once said, "my mind is cleansed when I walk in the snow."

During the Moscow phase of his life, he was able to come home to Japan once or twice a year. His visits were always unexpected because he came home whenever he was not busy and could take the time to leave. I always looked forward to these surprise visits and was always delighted to see him. Chiune embraced the Russian way of life so well that he was sometimes critical of Japanese ways. For example, he preferred the Russian way of drinking tea to the Japanese way. While the Japanese usually drink their tea in tiny cups which were never filled to the top, the Russians had their tea in large glasses called *skatun* which they filled to the very top. In fact, they usually filled the *skatun* to overflowing, so that the overflow spilled into saucers. Then they drank from the saucers when their glass was emptied. He also disliked the way Japanese had a tendency to walk in lines whenever they were in groups. He felt that their style of walking in lines reflected upon their lack of ability to be spontaneous and to relax. He believed that Japanese people needed to learn to be more uninhibited and become more natural. Chiune was also disappointed with the behavior of Japanese travelers to Moscow. He was critical of their tendency to belittle the Russians in loud voices while speaking in Japanese, and assuming that the Russians couldn't understand them. The Japanese were becoming economically more powerful and Chiune felt that they were also beginning to behave arrogantly. Their display of poor manners caused many Russians to feel resentful. Chiune felt sad and disappointed by this because he had always believed that people judged foreigners by their behavior while visiting a country. Chiune did not like what he was seeing in Moscow.

In 1964, Kawakami Trading Company was purchased by Chori Incorporated in a takeover. However, he continued to work for Chori and was later assigned to be in charge of a plant that exported big sewing machines to the Soviet Union.

Chapter 7

Reunion

A Sudden Telephone Call

IN AUGUST OF 1968, during one of Chiune's rare surprise visits home from the Soviet Union, he received a telephone call at about noon from the Israeli Embassy. Soon after the call he visited the Embassy. When Chiune returned that evening, he was in a very animated and excited mood rather than in his usual calm and composed state. When he saw me, he said, "I was surprised today. One of the Jewish refugees to whom I had issued a visa, a Mr. Nishri, came to Japan. He is an economic attaché of the Israeli Embassy." I was stunned to hear this news of a survivor. "He's an attaché now?" I asked. "And he's alive and safe?"

Twenty-eight years had passed since that unforgettable day in Kaunas. I recalled that Mr. Nishri was one of the five Jewish representatives chosen to enter the Consulate to discuss their desperate situation. Chiune continued to describe this surprise meeting as he told me what happened. Apparently Mr. Nishri showed Chiune a piece of paper and asked, "do you remember this?" That piece of paper was the very same visa that Chiune had issued to him 28 years ago. It was now a very old and worn out piece of paper. Mr. Nishri treasured it until the day he died.

As I listened to Chiune's account of the meeting, I experienced a multitude of emotions, such as surprise, astonishment, relief and happiness, to discover that at last there was

Visas for Life

indeed a survivor. Several days later, we went to visit Mr. Nishri at the Israeli Embassy. The meeting was very emotional, and we could not control the tears welling up in our eyes as we held one another's hands tightly. Mr. Nishri told us that many Jewish survivors who had received visas from Chiune had tried to locate him since the end of the war. Until now, the search had been in vain. They sought information at the Japanese Foreign Ministry, but no information was forthcoming. No one seemed to remember or recognize the name Sugihara.

Chiune had told the refugees to call him "Sempo," which is another name for "Chiune" in Japanese, and is also easier to pronounce. To the refugees, Chiune was known as Sempo Sugihara. It could have been that the Japanese Foreign Ministry did not recognize "Sempo" as being the "Chiune" they had in their records. However, I was aware that there were only three Sugiharas registered in the Kasumegaseki Register, which is a registry of former diplomats. The ministry should have known that only one of them was the Sugihara who had been Consul of Kaunas. I felt that the failure to find Chiune had less to do with a misunderstanding, and more to do with a lack of cooperation by the Japanese government. The Jews who were looking for Chiune might have been faced with the many layers of bureaucracy that exist in Japan.

Some time earlier Chiune had become curious about the fate of the Jewish refugees who had received his visas, so he went to make inquiries at the Israeli Embassy. Since the embassy personnel had no information to give him at the time, Chiune left his address there in case some information eventually turned up. When Mr. Nishri made inquiries at the Israeli embassy, he was able to contact Chiune because he'd left his address there years before. This joyful reunion, which took place after 28 long years, was truly a blessing. Chiune never mentioned being fired by his government for issuing the visas.

The reunion was especially momentous for Chiune because he had not known for all those years whether or not his decision to sign the visas resulted in saving any lives. But now that he knew there were many survivors, there was no doubt in his mind that the decision he had made was worth every hardship he had endured. Had he only saved one life, Chiune still would have felt it was worth the struggle.

Reunion

That same year, 1968, our youngest son Nobuki, who was of college age, was invited by Hebrew University in Israel to enroll as a foreign exchange student. Nobuki received a full scholarship because of Chiune's actions in Lithuania.

As more people became aware of Chiune and the incident in Kaunas, our lives became more active and public. The Asahi newspaper wrote an article on August 2, about Chiune titled "A Benefactor for 4,000 Jewish Refugees." The following year while Chiune was still working in Moscow, he was invited by the Kaunas survivors to visit Israel. Zorach Warhaftig, who was the Israeli government's Minister of Religion, and had signed the Israeli Declaration of Independence, was on hand to welcome my husband.

Warhaftig, who has 25 grandchildren, called my husband an 'emmisary of God.'

Warhaftig took Chiune to Yad Vashem. Yad Vashem is a beautiful museum with an archive of names of those killed in the Holocaust. It has a memorial Hall of Remembrance, a place to mourn Jews killed in the Holocaust. There is also a section to honor and praise those who helped save Jews during the Holocaust. An "Eternal Flame" burns quietly in the Sanctuary of Reminiscence. The names of 22 death camps that

Chiune with Sugihara survivor Zorach Warhaftig, Religious Minister of Israel, 1969.

were operated by the Nazis such as Auschwitz, Treblinka, Bergen-Belsen, and Dachau are engraved on the sanctuary floor.

Chiune recalled that one inscription at Yad Vashem said, "To remember and never forget." Chiune could easily relate to this inscription, as he always remembered the day we left Kaunas. He recalled that as the train was leaving the station, the Jewish people ran along the side of the train and shouted, "We will not forget you!" How well he now knew that these people did not forget him.

During this visit to Israel, Chiune was a guest of the vice mayor of Tel Aviv, Sofi Krementenoski. In Tel Aviv, he was given a tour of some of the city's historic sites. They also visited the site of a proposed medical center. There was a plan to build a five-story building, which would contain medical equipment that could possibly be purchased from Japan. Chiune was asked to negotiate the purchase of this equipment. However, because he was still living in Moscow and returning to Japan only once or twice a year, he regretfully declined this position. While Chiune was still in Israel, he took the opportunity to visit with Nobuki. He was pleased to discover that although Nobuki had initially had some difficulty mastering Hebrew, he had overcome this problem. Nobuki had also learned to speak Yiddish. He was enjoying his life in Israel with his many new friends.

When Chiune returned to Moscow, he did not talk about his visit to Israel or say anything about all the tributes that were bestowed upon him. His friends and colleagues were not aware of what Chiune had done. Chiune preferred quietly to enjoy the satisfaction of knowing that people had remembered him, and that they had showed their appreciation for what he had done.

Another survivor who came back into our lives was Joseph Shimkin, who lived in Shanghai after his escape from Kaunas. He later resided in Japan and owned a trading company there. He visited with Chiune several times, and these visits were the beginning of a lifelong friendship between the two men.

Chiune also had the opportunity to meet with the daughter of Franz, who had been a houseboy at the Japanese Consulate in Königsberg. He ran into her in London on his way back to Moscow from Israel. Franz's daughter was only a child in

1940, but she remembered Chiune and expressed great joy upon meeting him again. She recounted her experiences in Königsberg after the Soviet occupation. She told Chiune that the Germans, who had occupied Königsberg, had treated her family very badly and that they had later been forced to leave.

During the 15 years that Chiune was living in Moscow, I adjusted my life to being alone. I wrote my *tankas,* and taught flower arrangement. I even began learning about *noh* drama and its musical accompaniment. Since I had the chance to learn many new things, I led an interesting life. My life at this point was a peaceful and content one.

Chiune began to experience heart problems while he was still working for the trading company in Moscow. In 1976, he finally decided to retire and to return to Japan. When he returned, we sold our house in Kugenuma, which was now too large for just the two of us. After selling the house, we bought another in Kamakura, close to Kamakura Mountain. There we enjoyed taking walks. One of my fondest recollections of our life in Kamakura is that of hearing Chiune play his favorite musical piece, "A Maiden's Prayer," on the piano.

Nobuki (right) and Chiune, Israel, 1969. Nobuki received a full scholarship to Hebrew University in recognition of his father's deeds.

The Golden Hill

The year 1985 was memorable and important for us. In that year we were notified that Chiune was chosen to receive the "Righteous Among Nations" Award from Yad Vashem. It was to be awarded to him by the Israeli government. This award is given to non-Jews who helped save Jewish people during the Holocaust. It is an award that is held in the highest esteem. Hundreds of people in the world have received this honor. Chiune was the only Japanese citizen to receive this prestigious award. Chiune was also the first and only Asian to be recognized by Yad Vashem.

By now, Chiune's health had deteriorated to the extent that it was impossible for him to attend the ceremony. On January 18, 1985, Hiroki and I went on his behalf to receive the award. This was awarded to him at the Israeli Embassy in Tokyo. This event was reported worldwide. It was covered by newspapers in the United States, France, and Japan. It was reported on German radio stations, in virtually all Japanese newspapers and on Japanese television stations. Chiune played down this worldwide interest by the media by saying, "it's not as important as they treat it." The majority of the public agreed that this recognition given to Chiune was long overdue. My husband's response to his sudden renown can be best expressed by what he said to me. He looked at me seriously and said, "what I did as a diplomat who disobeyed his country's orders while serving his government may have been wrong, but I could not, in good conscience, ignore the pleas of thousands of people who sought my help. Therefore, I conclude that I did the only right thing, as any decent human being would have done. In the end, history will be the true judge."

We received many letters as a result of all the media coverage we were getting. Most of the letters were in praise, expressing respect for Chiune's decision. Many of them also expressed outrage about his dismissal from the Japanese Foreign Ministry. There were even several requests for his autograph. Not all of the letters were warm, because he did receive some unfriendly letters from people who thought that his was an act of insubordination against his country. I felt that those critics were unable to comprehend the spirit of Chiune's act.

Chiune had actually been honored by the Jewish community of Tokyo two weeks before he received this worldwide publicity. He had received an invitation from the Israeli Embassy to attend a reception that was held at the Jewish Community Center in Tokyo on January 6, 1985. The reception was to welcome Yitzak Shamir, who was soon to be the Prime Minister of Israel. Japanese Prime Minister Yasuhiro Nakasone had invited Shamir to a meeting in Japan so that stronger ties could be developed between the two countries. Even though Chiune's health had begun to deteriorate, he had a strong desire to attend this meeting while he was still capable of walking on his own two feet. He also expressed a strong desire to once again meet with Mr. Nishri and Ambassador Ben Yohanon, whom he had not seen for a long time. In his weakened condition, Chiune needed my support to help him walk.

We arrived at the Jewish Community Center in Tokyo, and were instantly surrounded by many Jewish people. Among the crowd was the familiar face of Joseph Shimkin, who had by now become our very close friend. There were the many faces of people we did not recognize. They introduced themselves

Chiune and Tsuru Kikuchi (Yukiko's mother) and their friends from Sacramento, California, in front of Sugihara's house in Kugenuma.

Visas for Life

Yitzak Shamir, Israeli Foreign Minister (future Prime Minister), in Tokyo, 1985.

to us as survivors from Kaunas who had received visas from Chiune. Ambassador Ben Yohanon requested that Chiune be seated next to him, and he eloquently expressed in a speech his appreciation for what Chiune had done in Kaunas. It was an unforgettable and rewarding, yet very tiring day, for Chiune. He was constantly delayed by reporters who requested interviews and asked him many questions.

In November 1985, a monument to honor Chuine's beneficent act was erected on a hill in Jerusalem. A dedication was held at Beit Shemesh in conjunction with a tree planting ceremony. Chiune's physical condition had progressively worsened, so it was impossible for him to attend. Nobuki was chosen to go to this event on behalf of his father. Since Israel is a desert country, plants and trees are highly treasured. Tree planting is regarded as very important and significant. A cherry tree was originally selected for the planting. That decision was later changed to a cedar tree because cedar is more sturdy and can better withstand the harsh desert soil. The change was significant because Sugihara literally means "cedar grove." Cedar is considered one of the holiest of woods because it was used to build the first Jewish Temple.

Reunion

Thirty cars and buses formed a stately procession that led up a hill to Beit Shemesh, carrying all the people attending the ceremony. Nobuki sent us a letter describing his experience and the event:

> "Today was the most beautiful day of my life! Against the backdrop of a clear blue sky, the Japanese flag with the Rising Sun and the Israeli flag with the star of David, flew side by side in friendship. The tree ceremony began at Beit Shemesh, which is located at the outskirts of Jerusalem. This was also the site of intense fighting, where many lives were lost during Israel's war for independence. The tree planting ceremony lasted about one and a half hours. Ten cedar trees were planted for the occasion. A special platform was built for the dedication of Father's monument.
>
> "The ceremony began with words of congratulations by a Knesset member. Then Zorach Warhaftig, a Jewish representative from Lithuania, spoke. Mr. Kohashi, the program director, had brought cedar trees to the site and he also spoke. There were over 70 visa recipients there that day. The survivors came to congratulate me one by one. One said, 'We were saved by Mr. Sugihara and we now have thirty grandchildren.' There were many other heartfelt comments such as, 'My parents, brothers, sisters, and relatives live all over the world,' or 'Please give our best to your great and brave father. I hope he gets better soon,' and others asked, 'How is your mother? Is she still in good health?' Some made comments like, 'The plight of the Jews in Lithuania was terrible.' An older blonde woman said, 'I was the only woman waiting at the fence of the Japanese Consulate. Your father sent a messenger to tell me that he understood how difficult it was for me and that he would issue a visa for me the next day. I was able to go home and rest. I thought that he was a real gentleman. I still have that visa.'
>
> "I thought that the handshaking would never end, although I really didn't mind it because I sensed the deep appreciation they all felt as I looked into their eyes. I felt very proud and happy to have such great parents. Finally, the evening came upon us as the clear blue sky turned to

Medal from Yad Vashem, "Righteous Among Nations," 1985.

> what is referred to as 'Golden Jerusalem.' This was the end of a glorious day for me."

As I read Nobuki's letter to Chiune, his eyes filled with tears of joy. We felt genuine happiness in our hearts because we knew that our children had realized and understood what we had done. We felt the pride our children had for their father for what he had done in Kaunas. It was also heart-warming for us to know that so many people took the time to attend the ceremony.

After graduating from the Hebrew University, Nobuki decided to remain in Israel. He was now fluent in Hebrew. He worked for a jewelry company for a while, and then decided to start his own business. With the help of many of his Jewish friends, he started his own business. He eventually expanded and established a jewelry factory in Thailand, with an office in Antwerp, Belgium. Nobuki confided to me that he never openly told anyone who his father was. On some occasions, when someone would ask if he happened to know about Chiune Sugihara, he would answer, "he is my father." They would usually react enthusiastically. Many times, they would convey a feeling of awe and tearfully show excitement and joy in meeting his son.

As Chiune's health declined in 1984, he was bedridden. Chiune had worked until the age of 75. He was a strong man and had survived the harsh, cold climate of Moscow even in

Reunion

his old age. He chose to work in his advanced years rather than lead a more sedentary life because he had always been an energetic and active person. As Chiune's condition worsened, he suffered several heart attacks. Throughout his illness, he remained his strong, stoic self, and never complained about his pain. On occasion, Chiune would sometimes ask that I hold his hand until he fell asleep.

On the morning of July 29, 1986, as Chiune was having breakfast, he expressed a desire to chat with me. He looked at me and said, "Yukiko, you have lived up to my every expectation. You have been the best." I then jokingly asked, "whom do you compare me with?" He answered, "I never compared you with anyone. What I wanted to say is that being married to you has been wonderful." He also wanted me to know that he was very sincere about everything he was saying. This was our last real conversation.

Shortly, I went back upstairs to check on him and to give him his favorite snack of sweet red bean soup with rice cakes and tea. He was sleeping, but I became alarmed because his sleep seemed unusually deep. I felt apprehensive and quickly went next door to ask a neighbor, who was a doctor, to check on him. The doctor advised that he should immediately be sent to the hospital in an ambulance. Chiune did not awaken from his deep slumber that night. The next morning, the doctor urged me to go home and get some rest. He assured me that his condition was not critical. Hiroki's wife, Michi, took over my bedside vigil. While she was there, he suddenly awoke and noticed that he was in an unfamiliar place. He asked, "Where is Yukiko?" Michi answered, "she went home, but she will be back very soon." With those words of assurance, Chiune fell asleep again.

The next morning he left us for Heaven. His life had passed away, and I noticed the shimmer of the mid-summer sea, which Chiune loved, reflecting through the window.

With the news of Chiune's passing, the Israeli Ambassador, Yaacov Cohen, came to pay his respects at our home. He brought with him an official message of condolence from the Israeli government. We received hundreds of telegrams of condolence from all over the world. Among the 300 or more people in attendance at the funeral were former classmates and students from Harbin Gakuin, and friends from the Soviet

Medal from Israeli government.

Union. There was even a stranger dressed in the manner of a manual laborer who came to offer his condolences. When I invited him into my home, he declined the invitation, as he said that he had to get back to work. He left without even telling me his name. He gave me an envelope. His offering contained a neatly folded 1,000 yen bill. We humbly accepted his gift with gratitude and appreciation. Chiune lay in peaceful repose as the music he had requested played through our home. His ashes were laid to rest at Kamakura Cemetery.

We received many more letters and words of condolence from people who could not attend the funeral. Mr. Zell, who had passed through Kaunas, lived in the United States and was at that time bedridden. He sent his regret that he could not attend the funeral. He has since died. I later heard that when Mr. Zell discovered that Chiune had been dismissed from the Foreign Ministry because of the incident in Kaunas, he was very offended and vowed to send a strong complaint to the Ministry. There were many others who expressed the very same sentiment. Some of those people were rabbis, journalists, and world leaders. Chiune once said to me,

"I didn't do anything special that people have to talk about. I made my own decisions, that's all. I followed my own conscience and listened to it."

Friends All Over the World

Long after Chiune's passing, we still continued to receive letters from all over the world. In April 1989, I was invited to visit the Mir Yeshiva in Brooklyn. Since I now had even more time to myself, I accepted the invitation to go to New York. I was accompanied by Hiroki. Many of the people who were there to welcome us were refugees who had received visas in Kaunas. They all greeted us with tears in their eyes as memories of those days came back to them. I felt as though I was having a reunion with dear, long-lost friends. We were told about the yeshiva synagogue's plans to build a memorial hall. They requested that I give them information about Chiune's decision to issue the visas. I gave them many details about the frustrations he experienced before he arrived at his decision to issue the visas.

After our visit to New York, we went to Boston, where we had received many invitations and requests for a visit. There were hundreds of people in attendance at the Boston event. We met Kitty Dukakis and received many souvenirs and a Certificate of Commendation from the City of Boston. Hiroki spoke before the large crowd and told them his father's story. After the event, a Japanese couple who had never before heard of this incident came to speak with us. They told us that Chiune's story brought tears to their eyes. The couple was the Japanese Consul and his wife assigned to Boston. When we further explained the details of Chiune's life, they were dismayed that they had never heard his heartwarming story. Obviously, Chiune's story was a forgotten one in the Japanese Foreign Ministry.

Many of the survivors we met on this trip still had their old visas. It seemed that many of them still treasured that precious old piece of paper. As I looked more closely at the old visas, I noticed Chiune's writing was all distorted and did not look like his writing at all. It looked as if it were written by a different person. I believed this was a true reflection of the pain my husband had undergone as he continued to write visa after visa.

Since Hiroki had completed his education in the United States, he wanted to take this opportunity to visit his many friends around the country. I decided to go on my own to visit

Mrs. Zell, with whom I had been corresponding for some time. I looked forward to our meeting. She held onto my hand for a long time and would not let it go. We talked to each other in her beautiful home along Lake Michigan, and she told me about the hardships she and her family had endured before she finally arrived in the United States.

Mrs. Zell explained that when the refugees finally reached Japan, they were treated kindly by the Red Cross and the Church of His Holiness of Kobe. They were also aided by the Joint Distribution Committee. Those survivors who reached Japan stayed in Kobe, and from there they went to Shanghai, China. After the war, they eventually immigrated around the world. The Zell family settled in the United States. After a period of many hardships, Mr. Zell started his own jewelry company. The Zells' daughter was only three years old when the family arrived in Kaunas, so her recollections of that time are not very clear.

Chiune Sugihara.

I learned that Jewish families value lessons learned from stories and experiences. These stories are passed down from one generation to the next so that they will never be forgotten. Mrs. Zell even wrote a book about her family's escape from Poland and the problems they overcame in the United States. On the other hand, many of the experiences suffered by Jewish refugees were so terrible and beyond imagination, that many survivors prefer not to talk about these memories. They are much too painful to even think about.

As interest in Chiune's life continued to increase all over the world, an interest also began to take hold in Japan. Many people thought that this was long overdue. Had Chiune still been alive, he would have said that receiving the Yad Vashem award was all the satisfaction he would ever need. He intensely disliked being interviewed by journalists. He would have preferred to remain anonymous. Japan has built a Memorial Park and monument to Chiune in Yaotsu, which is his place of birth. Property for the park and Memorial Hall were donated by the town of Yaotsu. A statue in his honor has also been erected. If Chiune were alive and knew of all of these honors, he would be extremely embarrassed about all this attention.

Worn-Out Visas

The Polish refugees who received visas from Chiune were very fortunate. However, they still had many dangers and hardships to face before they reached safety. These visas did not guarantee their safety as they had to travel through the vast lands of the Soviet Union. Although anti-Semitism was not an official policy of the Soviet Union, the country had basically been strongly anti-Semitic since the time of Czarist Russia Traveling across Russia was a long trip fraught with dangers and uncertainty.

A war between Russia and Germany was imminent. As dangerous as the trip to Vladivostok was, in the event of war, the dangers would increase a hundred-fold. The situation would be further complicated if, as rumored, Germany were to invade Lithuania. To avoid being trapped by all these circumstances, it was imperative that the refugees flee Kaunas as soon as possible. Those who had the money were able to leave quickly. But most refugees had escaped Poland with literally just the shirts on their backs. Many of them had arrived in wagons hidden under straw. Many had suffered the indignity of being poked with sharp rakes as these wagons were inspected.

Jewish groups in the United States formed an organization called the Joint Distribution Committee for the purpose of helping the Jews escape. This organization negotiated with tourist bureaus in Japan and in the Soviet Union and came up with an agreement. Under the conditions of the agreement, the Joint Distribution Committee was to guarantee travel expenses for the refugees. It was decided that the Soviet Union National Travel Agency, Intourist, would handle the Siberian Line; while the Japan Tourist Bureau would handle the trip from Vladivostok to the United States. All of the tickets were to be paid in advance. The cost of the ticket for the Siberian Line was $200 U.S. dollars. This price was about 15 times the cost of an ordinary fare. It is believed the Japanese government agreed to these plans because it was important at this time to ease tensions between Japan and the United States.

As the refugees got on their trains from Kaunas, it was so overcrowded that people could not even move. Every time they arrived at a station, someone had to send someone ahead to check if it was safe to go further. It was necessary to develop a safety check because everyone realized that they were traveling through unfriendly territory. If they received a message indicating that the train preceding them had arrived safely, they all would go back on their train and continue the trip. This happened at each train stop. It is no wonder that this trip usually took over two weeks. After the train from Lithuania finally reached Minsk or Moscow, it would continue on to Vladivostok.

The refugees on this train were treated harshly. When the train finally reached Vladivostok, only those who had entry permits or destination papers were allowed to continue. The same instructions held true in Manchuria where many Polish refugees had gone. Because so many people needed to get their entry permits, there were crowds of refugees daily at the Japanese Consulate in Vladivostok waiting to get their papers. Mr. Mei was the Acting Japanese General Consul there. He was a graduate of Harbin Gakuin and he knew Chiune very well. With the rush of refugees requesting entry visas, the situation was becoming chaotic. Mr. Mei cabled the Japanese Foreign Ministry recommending that since it was impossible to send the refugees who did not have proper papers back to Kaunas, it would behoove the Japanese government to accept them without papers. He also implied that not doing so was to risk losing the confidence of other countries.

A contract was drawn up between the Joint Distribution Committee and the Japan Travel Bureau to set up a schedule for the ship Harbin Maru to go once a week between Vladivostok and Tsuruga. The Harbin Maru was a small ship, so it rolled very badly whenever it hit the big waves on the Japan Sea.

Despite the discomforts, cold, seasickness, and crowded conditions experienced on this ship, there were cheers of joy expressed by the refugees as they left Soviet territory. Because the refugees had been treated harshly on the Siberian trains, their feeling was that the discomforts on the Japanese ship were negligible. The first group to arrive at Tsuruga landed on November 6, 1940. When everyone finally arrived in Tsuruga, Japan, their next stop was Kobe. The refugees continued onto their final destinations from Kobe or Yokohama. Most of them were sent to Shanghai. A few fortunate refugees were able to go to the United States, Canada, England, South America, Australia. and Palestine. The opportunity to arrange travel for the refugees by the shipping companies and the travel agencies proved beneficial for them since domestic travel at this time was practically non-existent.

Each of the five representatives that were chosen to speak with Chiune in Kaunas left for different destinations after they arrived safely in Japan. As I have mentioned before, Zorach Warhaftig went to Israel. He became the Minister of Religion wrote a book about his escape. Yehoshua Nishri, who became our very special friend, was the person who made the first contact with Chiune after 28 years. He resided in Japan as an economic attaché. He also established a trading company in Tel Aviv. Another spokesman was Zvi Klementynovsky, a former vice- mayor of Tel Aviv who was retired and now lives with his family in Israel. Mr. Joseph Ogur owns a big hotel called the Hotel Savoy in Frankfurt. He has since sent me a card with the message, "please visit me."

A few of the refugees remained in Japan. Joseph Shimkin was one of those. Whenever Joseph talks about the past, a look of great sadness shadows his face. He told me that he was one of the thousand Jewish refugees who took the very last ship to Japan from Vladivostok in June of 1941. Prior to his trip across the sea to Japan, it had taken him ten months to get out of the Soviet Union. Mr. Shimkin lived in Poland when the persecutions began. As the situation worsened, he decided to became a member of the Joint Distribution Committee that also helped refugees escape from Germany and other parts of Europe as well as from the Soviet Union. Born in 1905, he was 34 years old at this time. In September 1939, the Nazis invaded Poland, and some Jewish people began their escape to Lithuania. While engaged in helping his fellow countrymen flee, he became concerned about his family back in Poland. His concern prompted him to return there three times. Needless to say, each return trip to Poland was fraught with danger. Tragically, his return was too late because his family had been taken away. Joseph Shimkin could not find out where they had been sent. When I inquired about the fate of his family, he closed his eyes and kept silent for a while. Then he finally found the strength to continue telling me his story in a low, controlled voice. He said, "my parents, my wife, a five year old son, a seven-year-old daughter, my brothers, and many other relatives- my whole family- all 23 of them were killed. Only I survived because I left Poland to work with the Joint Distribution Committee." The awful irony and tragedy of his story left me speechless and I just kept listening to him quietly.

Mr. Shimkin also told me that after our family had left Kaunas at the end of August 1940, many more Jewish refugees continued flowing into the city. Since these refugees still needed visas, he devised a fake seal of the Japanese Consulate just like the seal used by Chiune. As a result of using that fake seal, over a hundred more lives were saved. A small smile returned to his face, as he revealed the fact that it was now safe for him to tell this part of his story because the statute of limitations for the forgery had passed. This little piece of his story brought a sense of relief and satisfaction to my heart because it eased the pain which I often suffered whenever I recalled the faces of the refugees we could not help.

He continued to encounter many more roadblocks in his life. Although he was instrumental in helping other refugees escape, he himself had a difficult time getting to America. Visas were needed at that time to travel anywhere. Since it was well known that he worked for the Joint Distribution Committee, he was called into the Soviet Union office in Kaunas and was interrogated and investigated daily for three weeks. A Lithuanian professor who worked in the Soviet Union office discreetly handed him an envelope as he was leaving the office one day. The envelope contained most of the papers needed to make his escape, but it did not have a visa in it. Joseph asked the Joint Distribution Committee for advise on how to get a visa and they told him that the American Embassy in Moscow would issue a visa to him for America when he arrived in Moscow. Mr. Shimkin boarded a train in Kaunas for Moscow. Upon reaching his destination the American Embassy said that it had not received any information about him so they did not have the authority to issue him a visa. He was only allowed to stay in Moscow three days, so he had to leave for Vladivostok without one. In Vladivostok, he received his traveling papers from the American Consulate. He was again told that he should go to Japan where he would receive his visa at the American Embassy in Tokyo. He no longer needed his visa for Curacao. He gave that visa to a friend. He finally arrived at the Port of Tsuruga on the last boat in June of 1941. Upon his arrival, he discovered that the Japanese government still refused to allow the refugees that did not have their destination papers in order to disembark. To avoid being sent back, Joseph stayed hidden in the ship for three days. About 70 refugees did not have their papers. When it was discovered that the Soviets were now refusing to allow anyone back into their country, the Japanese government finally relented and allowed them to disembark in Japan. From Tsuruga, Joseph went on to Kobe. He began to work for the Joint Distribution Committee again. It was several months before the war between Japan and the United States. For various reasons, it was still not possible for Mr. Shimkin to obtain a visa to leave Japan for America. He decided to leave Japan for Shanghai.

He lived in Shanghai for 14 years, where he imported chemical products. Just as his business was blossoming, the Communists took over in 1949. It then took him six long years

Visas for Life

to leave Communist ruled Shanghai. He gave everything he had worked for to the Chinese Communists to get a visa to go to Hong Kong. From Hong Kong, he left for Israel. He wanted to visit Japan again, and was able to obtain a visa from the Israeli government in 1956. Since his return to Japan, he had also looked for Chiune. They were finally reunited. Theirs was a friendship which developed in Kaunas. It continued until my husband's death in 1986. Their relationship endured through all the difficult times and years. It is this kind of enduring friendship which I would like to see develop between races and nations. It was friendship based on love and understanding that we are one and the same.

As for myself, I have come to believe that it is important to tell people about what Chiune did and for what he stood. I want to share this story with people all over the world because what he did was something that everyone should be able to do. They should listen to their conscience and find the courage to follow the right path. For my husband and me, it was our greatest delight to meet the people who treasured Chiune's act, which he saw as only natural.

Today, we seem to live in a confused era. War can be miserable, and people should educate themselves about other people's experiences. Today, anti-Semitism exists in Japan and elsewhere. I believe most people want peace. But there will be no peace until we have rid ourselves of all racism.

I have only one very strong wish. I do not want wars on earth. Wars should be eliminated. They bring nothing but misery to human beings. We really should forget our racial prejudice. We should set aside our discrimination in order to bring in genuine peace to this world. Peace is so precious. War is so ugly. It brings such chaos and misery.

Young people have to face what happened during the war. They cannot avoid history. We must tell young people what we went through, and how we suffered. We have an obligation to communicate what we know, to pass it on. If young people's awareness becomes heightened, they can do something to avoid wars and bring on peace. Soon it will be their world. They have to protect their future. I believe we can have a better world.

If my story, my personal experience, can help young people understand the need for peace on a personal level, I do not mind sharing my personal feelings. If people can learn from my stories, I will tell them until the last day of my life in this world.

Appendix, November 1995

ON AUGUST 12, 1992 a monument to my husband was dedicated in the town of Yaotsu, where Chiune was born, near the city of Nagoya. This beautiful monument is in the shape of a bamboo pipe organ. The monument sits in a lotus pond. The lotus is a symbol of purity. The ripples in the pond symbolize the ripple effect of one pebble and its impact on the entire world. The Hill on which the monument is placed, overlooks Yaotsu and is called the Hill of Humanity.

The monument's dedication was attended by the following people: Noboru Takeshita, the former Prime Minister of Japan; Taku Kajiwara, the Governor of Gifu Prefecture; Hajime Sako, the Chairman of Taisei Construction, the builder of the monument; Masayoshi Arai, the Mayor of Yaotsu; the Ambassador of Israel; Zorach Warhaftig, an Israeli citizen who received a visa from my husband in Lithuania in 1940; Masatoshi Morita, a Vice President for Toyota; Takao Ikami of Central Park Company; and my son Hiroki. The monument was funded by Noboru Takeshita, Yaotsu Town, Gifu Prefecture, Taisei Construction, and Takao Ikami of the Central Park Company of Nagoya.

In September 1994 a group of "Sugihara survivors," their families, and friends made a pilgrimage to Japan to honor the memory of my husband. The survivors were accompanied by Japanese American veterans of both the 442nd Regimental Combat Team, and the 522nd Field Artillery Battalion. The 522nd helped liberate the Dachau concentration camp complex and the Dachau death march in Germany in May 1945. This trip to Japan was sponsored by the Holocaust Oral History Project of San Francisco, and the Japanese American Veterans of the Pacific War. The organizers of the trip were Lani Silver, Eric Saul, Noby Yoshimura and Harry Fukuhara. They brought with them a beautiful exhibit on Chiune and the Japanese American soldiers of World War II. It traveled in Japan for over a year. I was also reunited with Solly Ganor who as a little boy in Kaunas had invited Chiune and me to our first Chanukah Celebration.

This group came to re-dedicate my husband's monument. I was so pleased and happy to see 300 people attend the ceremony. Former Deputy Prime Minister Masaharu Gotada gave a wonderful speech. The words of Japanese Foreign Minister Yohei Kono were inscribed on a beautiful monument on the Hill of Humanity as a permanent part of the memorial.

This was the first time that such a high representative of the Japanese Government and even the Foreign Minister himself honored my husband.

A Harbin Gakuin monument was also constructed by their Alumni Group.

During this ceremony, held on a bright September afternoon, a beautiful red hawk slowly circled above, and watched. The red hawk reminded me of my husband's spirit. In my speech I said this was the happiest day of my life.

From the first pebble, a ripple effect is taking place. More and more people are learning about my husband's decision for life. The story of Kaunas and the visas is spreading out all over the world. I want to thank everyone who keeps this story alive.

— Yukiko Sugihara

Chiune Sugihara Chronology

1900 Born January 1 in Yaotsu Town, Gifu Prefecture. Second son of father Yoshimizu, and mother Yatsu (a family of five boys and one girl).
1907 Enters Kuwana Elemantary School. Transfers to Nakatsu, then to Furuwatari, Schools.
1912 Graduates with top honors from Furuwatari School. Enters Nagoya Daigo Chugaku (Junior & High School).
1917 Graduates High School. Fails Keijo University Medical School entrance exam.
1918 Enters Waseda University. Majors in English Literature.
1919 Passes Foreign Ministry Scholarship exam. Enters Harbin Gakuin (National University). Studies Russian.
1920 Drafted into Army for one year as Reserve Lieutenant.
1921 Yatsu Sugihara (Chiune's mother) dies.
1923 Graduates Harbin Gakuin (National University), China. Receives Top Honors.
1924 Appointed as clerk in the Harbin Japanese Embassy.
1930 Becomes professor at Harbin Gakuin University.
1932 Becomes Deputy Consul of Manchurian Government Foreign Ministry.
1933 Appointed Chief of Northern Manchurian Railroad Aquisition Office, by the Manchurian Government Foreign Ministry; as Section Chief of Russian & Planning.
1934 Resigns in protest of the ill treatment of the Chinese.
1935 Returns to Japan. Marries Yukiko Kikuchi.
1936 First son, Hiroki, born in September. Appointed to Japanese Embassy in Russia, Second class translator.
1937 Becomes translator for Japanese legation, Helsinki, Finland.
1938 Second son, Chiaki, born.
1939 Appointed Japanese Consul to Lithuania. Stationed at Kaunas (Kovno).
1940 Third son, Haruki, born. Chiune Sugihara issues visas to Polish refugees. Becomes Japanese Consul to Czechoslovakia, via Berlin.
1941 Becomes Consul General to Königsberg.
1942 Becomes Consul General to Romania.

Chronology

1945 End of World War II. Sugiharas imprisoned in Russan internment camp in Romania.
1946 Returns to Japan via Trans-Siberian railroad and Nakhodka port.
1947 Returns to Hakata port (Japan) on the Koan-Maru (ship). Settles in Fujisawa City, Kanagawa Prefecture (one hour from Tokyo). Third son, Haruki, dies. Works for World Peace Foundation.
1948 Setsuko Konuma (Kikuchi) dies.
1950 Employed by Tokyo, U.S.A., as General Manager of U.S. Military Post Exchange.
1951 Fourth son, Nobuki, born. Employed by U.S. Trading Company.
1952 Becomes Sanki Trade Executive.
1954 Becomes professor, Nikolai Russian Language School. Becomes translator, Japan Science & Technology Agency.
1957 Works for N.H.K. Broadcasting, International Section.
1960 Becomes Moscow Office Chief, Kawakami Trade Company and Chori Trade Company.
1965 Becomes executive Branch Manager, Kokusai Koeki Company, Moscow.
1968 Mr. J. Nishri, 'Sugihara survivor' finds Chiune.
1969 Chiune visits Israel; honored by Israeli Government. Nobuki receives full scholarship to Hebrew University
1976 Chiune Sugihara retires.
1984 Tree planting in Sugihara's honor in Israel.
1985 Receives "Righteous Among the Nations" award by Israel's Holocaust Memorial, Yad Vashem.
1986 Dies July 31, at 86 years of age.
1989 "Courage to Care Award" awarded by Anti-Defamation League, New York.
1990 "Raoul Wallenberg Award" awarded by Shaare Zedek Hospital of Jerusalem, New York. Yukiko Sugihara writes her autobiography.
1991 Mir Yeshiva School establishes "Sempo Sugihara Scholarship," Brooklyn. A street in Lithuania is named after Chiune Sugihara.
1992 The Hill of Humanity monument dedicated by Yaotsu Town, Chiune's hometown. Sugihara receives Nagasaki Peace Prize.

Visas for Life

1993 Yukiko visits United States Holocaust Memorial Museum. Visits Sugihara plaque there. Japanese high school applies Sugihara's story in an English textbook.
1994 Bar Ilan University opens a Sugihara Center. Sugihara survivors and their families visit Japan.
1995 Receives Holocaust Oral History Project award. Yukiko Sugihara visits Mir Yeshiva, Brooklyn, N.Y. Sugihara Exhibit opened at Simon Wiesenthal Museum of Tolerance. Honored by Steven Spielberg at Holocaust testimonial dinner, January. Yukiko Sugihara's autobiography "Visas for Life" published in French, Portugese, and English.

List of Sugihara Awards

Righteous Among Nations Award, from Yad Vashem Heroes and Martyr's Remembrance Authority, 1985

Courage to Care Award, from the Anti-Defamation League, 1989

Nagasaki Peace Prize

City of San Francisco Mayor's Proclamation, from Mayor Frank Jordan, August 21, 1994

United States Senate Letter of Appreciation, from Senator Daniel Akaka, September 28, 1994

Japanese Community and Cultural Center of Northern California and the San Francisco Nikkei Lions Club Award, November 16, 1994

Entry into the Congressional Record, read by Congresswoman Nancy Pelosi, January 20, 1995

United States Senate Letter of Appreciation, from Senator Barbara Boxer, January 22, 1995

United States Senate Letter of Appreciation, from Senator Dianne Feinstein, January 22, 1995

United States Congress Certificate of Special Recognition, from Congressman Tom Lantos, January 22, 1995

Certificate of Honor, from San Francisco Board of Supervisors, January 22, 1995

State of California, Senate Rules Committee Resolution, by Senators Quentin L. Kopp, Milton Marks, Leroy F. Greene, Maurice Johannessen, Patrick Johnston, Bill Lockyer, and Herschel Rosenblatt, January 22, 1995

California State Senate Certificate of Recognition, from Senator Milton Marks, January 22, 1995

United States Congress letter of appreciation, from Congressman Robert T. Matsui, January 24, 1995

Visas for Life

Governor Pete Wilson, State of California, letter of appreciation, January 24, 1995

Honorary plaque, presented to Mrs. Yukiko Sugihara by the Jewish Community of the Sacramento Region, January 24, 1995

Declaration of Chiune and Yukiko Sugihara Day, Los Angeles, California, by the County of Los Angeles Board of Supervisors, February 8, 1995

Commendation by the City Council of Los Angeles, California, by the County of Los Angeles Board of Supervisors, February 8, 1995

Proclamation of Appreciation, from Mayor Dee Hardisan, Torrance, California, February 8, 1995

Statement of Appreciation, from Robert Harris, President, Sacramento City College, California

Acknowledgements

Like the pebble in the pond I would like to thank the ever-widening circle of friends of Chiune Sugihara. As the circle gets wider the effect on the pond becomes deeper and more profound.

I would like to thank my mother, Yukiko Sugihara, Michi Sugihara, Chiaki Sugihara, Mari and Chihiro Sugihara, Madoka and Tsutomu Nakamura, Nobuki Sugihara, Naoki Sugihara, Yuri Mikami, Sir Edmund L. de Rothschild, Takeyuki Shimizu, Katsumasa Watanabe, Kyozo Okazawa, Yoshiyuki Kawashima, Hiroshi Sekiguchi, Yukio Matsuo, Anne Hoshiko Akabori, Solly and Pola Ganor, Takao Ikami, Hiroko Amano, Shozo Katsuta, Susan Blumen, Barbara Blumen, and Robert Blumen.

I would also like to thank the staff and volunteers of the Holocaust Oral History Project for their generous assistance in helping the Sugihara family keep the story of Chiune Sugihara alive. Special thanks to Lani Silver, Eric Saul, John Angell Grant, Bill Schwartz, Sean Simplicio, Gal Adam, Masami Kobayashi, Nancy Magidson, Judith Antelman, Naomi Fagan, Judith Backover, Jason Moss, Nigel French, Dan Stack, Judy Colligan, Peggy Coster, Ellen Szakal, Sandra Bendayan, Karen Amital, Tamar Reinin, Amy Fiske, Ruth Durling, Rita Gopstein, the Board of Directors, and other project friends and supporters.

Finally, I would like to thank Noby Yoshimura and Harry Fukuhara, Kiyoshi Kawai, Jack Brauns, Kelly Crabb, Hillel Levine, Janice Anita Humphreys, and the Simon Wiesenthal Museum of Tolerance, Anti Defamation League, Shaarre Zedek Hospital of Jerusalem.

— Hiroki Sugihara

The Sugihara legacy lives on...

Ryzak family, Sugihara descendants.   Photo: Ron Greene

Moshe Langer, Sugihara survivor.   Photo: Ron Greene

as the circle of friends becomes wider and wider

Prince Philip of England and Hiroki Sugihara, London, 1993.

Vice President Walter Mondale. U.S. Ambassador to Japan, September, 1994.

Sir Edmund L. de Rothschild (center), London, 1993.

Raul Wallenberg Award presented to Yukiko Sugihara by Ross Perot, New York, 1990.

Sugihara survivors and descendants, San Francisco, 1995.

Survivors meet Yukiko for the first time in 55 years.

Steven Spielberg honored Mrs. Sugihara at a ceremonial dinner in Los Angeles, January 1995.

Photo: Art Waldinger/ Simon Wiesenthal Center

Opening of the "Visas for Life" exhibit, Museum of Tolerance, January, 1995.

Mr. Takao Ikami explains to Mr. Eiji Toyota, the Chairman and President of Toyota Motor Company, the story of the Sugihara family.

Mr. Takao Ikami was a schoolmate of Chiune Sugihara. Central Park Company, Nagoya. 1993.

Mr. Berek Winter and his brother both received Sugihara visas.   Photo: Ron Greene

Sugihara survivor Jerry Milrod, from Lodz, Poland. 1944.

Jerry and Lydia Milrod, 1995.   Photo: Ron Greene

Sugihara Visas List. 1940

NN.	NATIONALITY	NAME	ENTRANCE or TRANSIT	DATE of VISE	SASHOOMIOU	BIKOO
237	POLNISCH	Chil KESTENBERG	TRANSIT	30/VII	2	
238	"	Josef OSKROMSKY	"	"	2	
239	"	Girsch KLEMENTOWSKY	"	"	2	
240	"	Moses GUTMAN	"	"	2	
241	"	Abram STEIN	"	"	2	
242	"	Uehuda LINDWASER	"	"	2	
243	"	Leib MANN	"	"	2	
244	"	Anatol HUFNAGEL	"	"	2	
245	"	Symi OBERMAN	"	"	2	
246	"	Julian GLASS	"	"	2	
247	"	Schabse STEIN	"	"	2	
248	"	Josef ALENBERG	"	"	2	
249	"	Chaim SZLADOWSKI	"	"	2	
250	"	Regina WOFSI	"	"	2	
251	"	Isak WOFSI	"	"	2	
252	"	Jan SPILREIM	"	"	2	
253	"	Aron KOHN	"	"	2	
254	"	Josef PRYWIN	"	"	2	
255	"	Moses STEIN	"	"	2	
256	"	Israel OBERMAN	"	"	2	
257	"	Leon FEIT	"	"	2	
258	"	Alice KRUKOWSKA	"	"	2	
259	"	Ginga MILGROM	"	"	2	
260	"	Szimin BERNSTEIN	"	"	2	
261	"	Kaspel TAUSK	"	"	2	
262	"	Abram TAUSK	"	"	2	
263	"	Ioek LEDERMAN	"	"	2	
264	"	Bernhard STEIN	"	"	2	
265	"	Wigdor SPIRO	"	"	2	
266	"	Bencion TOROWITSCH	"	"	2	
267	"	Jankel WAISFELD	"	"	2	
268	"	Julisz SCHLEICHER	"	"	2	
269	"	Felicia MUNZ	"	"	2	
270	"	Rudolf MUNZ	"	"	2	
271	"	Sara GRAFF	"	"	2	
272	"	Ignacy GRAFF	"	"	2	
273	"	Abram FUKIELAN	"	"	2	
274	"	Fain Lejzor MORDKOWICZ	"	"	2	
275	"	Frenkiel Benjamin-Wolf	"	"	2	
276	"	Frenkiel Majer-Szachna	"	"	2	
277	"	Michal GRYNSZTEIN	"	"	2	
278	"	Samson GORDON	"	"	2	
279	"	Rozalia GORDON	"	"	2	
280	"	Adam BRZEZINSKI	"	"	2	
281	"	Szepsel GORDON	"	"	2	
282	"	Perla FRENKIEL	"	"	2	
283	"	Ruwin GRYNSZTEJN	"	"	2	
284	"	Chaim GRYNSZTEJN	"	"	2	
285	"	Szymon FELDBLUM	"	"	2	
286	"	Rosa FELDBLUM	"	"	2	
287	Lithuanien	Jankielis ZIMONAS	"	"	2	
288	Polnisch	Marek SZPIGELMAN	"	"	2	
289	"	Isak SZPIGELMAN	"	"	2	
290	"	Maks Ginzberg	"	"	2	
291	"	Nikodem KOW	"	"	2	
292	"	Irena KOW	"	"	2	
293	"	Chawa SZMARAGD	"	"	2	
294	"	Csarna FEFER	"	"	2	
295	"	Marian PRZELOMSKI	"	"	2	
296	"	Edward Krukowski	?	"	2	
297	"	Mortcha BIRENBAUM	"	"	2	
298	"	Walter DEUTSCH	"	"	2	
299	"	Salomon-Boruch-Szmul	"	"	2	
300	"	Matan FLANCBEJCH	"	"	2	
301	"	Aleksandr SZTEJNBERG	"	"	2	
302	"	Szmul-Eliasz TAUB	"	"	2	
303	"	Mieczyslaw KAWA	?	"	2	
304	"	Henryk HARENBERG	"	"	2	
305	"	Wladyslaw LICHTENBAUM	"	"	2	
306	"	Mieczyslaw LICHTENBAUM	"	"	2	
307	"	Israel SPIRA	"	"	2	

"Sugihara's List" with the typewritten names of 2,193 Jews and their families. This list was discovered in the Gaimusho (Japanese Foreign Ministry) archives in 1994.

160

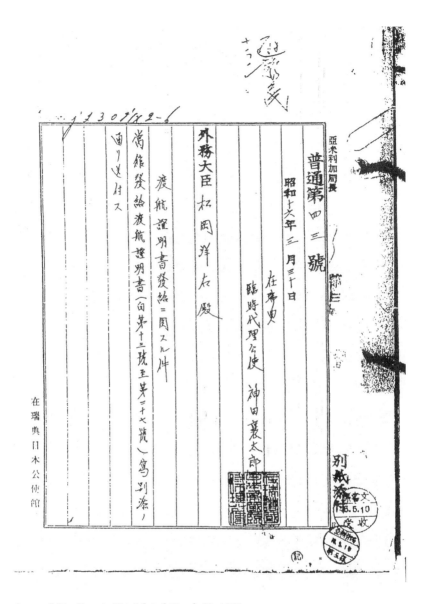

Cover of "Sugihara's List," dated March 30, 1946.

Chiune Sugihara's decision to issue visas may have been influenced by a 14-year-old Jewish boy named Solly Ganor. He invited Mr. Sugihara to celebrate the first night of Chanukah in 1939 with his family. This may have been Sugihara's first contact with a Jewish family in Kaunas.

Sugihara visa recipients, Kobe, Japan. May, 1941.

Harbin Gakuin. Sugihara graduated with honors in 1924 from this prestigious language school.

Kaunas Railway Station. Survivors left here for Russia, Japan and China.

Hotel Metropolis, Kaunas. Sugihara issued visas form this hotel just before he left for Berlin.

Former Japanese Consulate and Residence, 1993.
30 Weisgant Strasse, Kaunas, Lithuania.

Massacre of thousands of Lithuanian Jews. Ninth Fort, Kaunas, 1941.

Photo of mobile German murder squads who killed more than 15,000 Jews in three days. By the war's end, more than 94% of Lithuania Jews had been killed.

Mr. Sugihara died in Japan on July 31, 1986. A schoolmate, Mr. Takao Ikami and the town of Yaotsu built a large memorial and dedicated a park in remembrance of Chiune Sugihara. This is the dedication of the Sugihara monument in 1992. Yukiko Sugihara and eldest son, Hiroki, cut the ribbon, with ex-Prime Minister of Japan, Noboru Takeshita. Also pictured: Israeli Ambassador, Nahum Eshkol and the Mayor of Yaotsu, Masayoshi Arai.

The Sugihara memorial monument is built in the symbolic form of a bamboo-shaped peace organ in a pond. The pond symbolizes humanity, and the rings around it symbolize the ripple-effect of acts of kindness.

Kaunas, Lithuania, 1939.

*Chiune Sugihara,
January 1, 1900 –
July 31, 1986.*